Cw/cc

Thematic and Topical
STAMP COLLECTING

A practical and comprehensive
handbook for thematic,
topical and subject collectors

A. J. Branston

B. T. Batsford Ltd
London

ISBN 0 7134 1974 1

Printed in Great Britain by Redwood Burn Ltd,
Trowbridge and Esher
for the publishers, B. T. Batsford Ltd,
4 Fitzhardinge Street, London W1H 0AH

Contents

Acknowledgments

The author wishes to thank the following for their help: The Association of Scottish Philatelic Societies; Mrs Cornelia Austin; The American Philatelic Society and Writers Unit No. 30; Arthur Blair; Mrs Jean and Carrol Boyce; The Crown Agents Stamp Bureau for permission to reproduce certain stamps; Miss V. M. Clark; Mrs Carol Curtis; Mrs Elaine R. Durnin; Mrs G. Ebbage; Mrs Cleo Francisca; Joe E. Fry; *Gibbons Stamp Monthly Ltd*; Gustave Knockel; Ramon Goodey; Mrs S. Hall; Peter J. Hobday; the Jersey Postal Administration; Kenneth A. Wood; editor, *Stamp Collecting*; Miss Irene Lawford; Miss M. Mansfield; Christopher Rauch; W. A. Russell; J. C. Simmonds; The Smithsonian Institute, Franklin R. Bruns, Curator; M. J. Southall; J. Sullivan; *Stamp Collecting Ltd*; Stanley Gibbons Publications Ltd, for permission to reproduce catalogue numbers; Mrs Jean Swetland; Gary M. Trigwell; Barbara W. and Robert de Violini; Mrs Gwyneth Williams; and Lester Winick.

My special thanks are due to the following for the use of material and permission to reproduce it in this book: Mrs Margaret Jamieson; Mrs Margaret E. Morris; Jerome Husack of the American Topical Association; Ed Neuce of *Linns Stamp Weekly;* and Wonderlin's (USA).

Finally I express considerable gratitude to O. J. Simpson, BSc., FRIC, FCS for his patience and care in checking the manuscript and to Mrs V. Vohmann for typing it.

Alfred J. Branston

Preface

This is a book about a collecting activity which is becoming increasingly popular over most of the world. Although it has been written especially for new and existing collectors in Great Britain and America, it is equally invaluable for those in Europe and Australia.

This book is the first to appear in either Great Britain or America on the complete art and craft of thematic and topical collecting. It has not been written from the historical aspect for the simple reason that the author considers it is undoubtedly better that this new and ongoing subject should be treated with a forward outlook. It will therefore provide information and offer guidance which past experience and current practice indicate will be needed for today and tomorrow.

It recognises the important fact that the topical collections of the USA, and the thematic collections of Great Britain and the *motif* collections of Europe have one and the same collecting basis. When looked at objectively it is evident that these two activities spring from a single base in which they show marked similarities. It is therefore reasonable to hold that it is totally incorrect to regard topicals as one kind of collecting and thematics as quite another. In the light of this, it is hoped that all collectors whether in Great Britain, the USA or Europe will fully appreciate and accept that they all belong to one collecting family.

It is of note that quite a high proportion of the end products—the album pages—show little or no difference between one country and another. Today language differences no longer represent collecting barriers. Highlighting the minor contrasts which exist between thematics and topicals is not one of the objects of this book, nor does the author see that any good and and progressive purpose would be served by so doing.

From the start this book recognises that there are two basic principles of collecting. The first is that all collectors are free to set up and arrange their collections in precisely the way which pleases them the most. This freedom is inviolable and, accordingly, there is not the slightest need to defend, here or elsewhere, this or that way of collecting. The second principle concerns the purposes of collecting. Without regard to priorities of any sort, the objects are fun, pleasure, satisfaction, enthusiasm, incentive, relaxation and stimulation. The author considers it his job to see that the readers of this book are offered every possible opportunity to get their fair share. They can be secured in two ways. The easiest, of course, is to do the collecting in a way which directly produces the greatest amount of fun, pleasure and satisfaction. Avoiding pitfalls and difficulties makes progress far happier.

Here the author takes the opportunity not only to introduce a number of relatively new ideas but also an important positive concept. This is that we should recognise collectors, not according to their expertise, but according to the general nature of their collecting interests. Thus, the very large number of collectors who never enter the competitive world *and* those who regularly do so are catered for as equal components in the world of thematic and topical collecting.

Because it is a handbook and not a textbook, no attempt whatsoever is made to give instructions of any sort. However, when routines are offered or methods of finding answers to awkward collecting questions are suggested, there is certainly no lack of specific direction as to how they are to be applied or realistic solutions secured. In other words, this is a practical book.

It is in no sense a check list of the stamps and their background to be used so that a collection on a specific subject can be started. Nor has it any resemblance to any sort of catalogue, historical list and the like. It is, in fact, a radical departure from any such book.

Collecting is very much a matter of personal pleasure and satisfaction. The need to recognise a strict terminology ranks far below the requirements of satisfaction, fun and pleasure. Thus the terms 'thematic', 'topical' and 'subject' are used loosely on some occasions, but on others they refer to precisely defined classes of collection. These terms therefore have both generic and specific usages according to the circumstances of the user. The academic may well see a serious need for this dichotomy to be cleared up once and for all but the author carries no banner for reformation and special regulations. Those who enjoy thematic politics more than practical collecting are free to spend as much time as they wish on discussing and revising such basics as terminology and the like. Instead, the reader is offered a considerable amount of precise information on both the meanings and the usages of the terms 'topical', 'thematic' and 'subject' as applicable today.

Here is a thought about terminology. Because the words 'topical' and 'thematic' spring from the same basic activity it ought to be possible to replace them by a single descriptive name. This would not only be rational but also very convenient for usage in this book. It would undoubtedly be much to the advantage of the reader to have such a simple description and so be saved any annoyance from the frequent repetition of such phrases as 'in topical, thematic and subject types of collecting'. As an experiment, the author tried out a number of suitable words, including compounds, on collectors in the British Isles. None of those suggested found favour nor did any positive alternatives result. Avoiding the thought that collectors are not lexicographers, the best that emerged was the straight 'thematics/topicals'. For the sake of Anglo-American equality in this book, the term 'topical/thematic' will appear approximately the same number of times as does the reverse 'thematic/topical'. Prejudices are no part of collecting and it is hoped that this turn-and-turn-about arrangement will amply satisfy the pride of all such collectors in whatever country they reside.

This book neither says nor recognises that some subjects are simple to collect and that others are more difficult or even complex to set up satisfactorily. Complexity and difficulty are no part of happy collecting and it is therefore suggested that the collecting should be taken to a depth and degree of diversity which affords the owner the amount of satisfaction he needs—and no further.

Two new terms are introduced to the reader. Thematic

expertise can make an important contribution to progressive collecting. It is the ability to think through in order to produce the maximum amount of thematic/topical/subject progress in terms of completed pages or competitive entries. The other new term has an entirely different and more personal application. There are very many collectors and even more would-be collectors who wish to enjoy doing exactly as they wish in their collecting and are quite unable to accept the rules and disciplines of competitions. Despite many suggestions British collectors were unable to find a better name for this very popular type of collecting than 'non-competitive'. This negative is not entirely satisfactory and it would have been better if a name with a positive indication could be found. Until its emergence, the term non-competitive will have to be used. In this connection, this book has been designed to give equal, wide and practical coverage of both the competitive and the non-competitive areas of collecting. It deals first with the non-competitive type of collection for several reasons. There are many more collectors in the non-competitive area of collecting than in the competitive. Second, an entry to a competition or exhibition is in the nature of an extension to or extraction from a collection of the usual type. Next, the non-competitive type of collection is very wide in scope and diverse in character. By dealing first with this sort of collection a considerable amount of thematic ground has been covered in the early part of the book with advantage to the reader. Another point is that the amount of thematic and philatelic expertise required to produce a good non-competitive collection relates largely to the collector's personal capability. Some collectors make a point of employing their philatelic knowledge to the maximum whilst others find equal enjoyment without it. In the competitive area the priorities are much better defined. The continual pressure for 'better and better' calls for more and more expertise on the part of the entrant. The order in which this book deals with the two types of collection—non-competitive and competitive—is therefore the best for both types of reader. Lastly, in Great Britain, there is currently a dearth of organised information about non-competitive collecting and it is hoped that the information given will help to make good this deficiency.

Good thematic collecting, especially in the matter of competitions, requires not only the skills of good stamp collecting but also a sound working knowledge of philately. So a good collector needs to be a stamp collector first of all and a 'thematicist' thereafter.

Emphasising the importance of this order, the book suggests that the practical skills and background knowledge which are so vital should be acquired in two steps, the first before and the second during the actual work of assembling the thematic/topical/subject collection.

If starting the collection in the right way is important from the practical angle, then selecting the best subject for the individual to collect is even more so. This book deals extensively with the mechanics of theme and topical selection, how to make a satisfactory start and then to build up the collection so that it produces the maximum pleasure and satisfaction.

This book draws upon a number of collections arranged by the owners in Great Britain and in America, as examples of what each considers to be the ideal end product—the pages in a well-filled album.

The finance of collecting covers very much more than the job of selling the collection. Buying is undoubtedly a real part of collecting pleasure; it is also synonymous with collection building. The author suggests that when spending and pleasure are the main objectives, it is a good idea to know something about buying. The thoughts about this aspect of collecting have therefore been placed immediately before those about selection of the subject, collecting methods and collection building. Being wise after an event is often not a pleasant experience.

The lines of organisation of the competitive type of collecting in America differ considerably from those in Great Britain and are far more complex. The two chapters on local and federation competitions and on nationals of necessity are therefore rather general in character and the reader should interpret the information given to fit the particular circumstances.

Very recently there have been a number of important changes in the international areas of thematic exhibiting. These are just beginning to be reflected in competitions at lower levels. Such changes and their effects are explained at length in the later chapters of the book.

Opportunity has been taken in the early part of the book to explain some of the terms frequently used by American collectors and the Press. Many of these are as yet unknown in Great Britain.

This work is intended primarily for the adult collector who will already have, or is prepared to secure, a good working knowledge of all aspects of stamp collecting. The philatelically minded teenager should also find its ongoing outlook very encouraging. The author hopes that all readers will see in this book precisely what is needed to get each of them into the top flight of thematic collecting.

Introduction

Currently, collectors in the other branches of philately are agreed that it is the thematic/topical enthusiast who enjoys the maximum amount of freedom. This is because he can build his collection from a far wider range of material than they can and there is a real possibility, therefore, of his achieving a greater amount of pleasure and satisfaction than them. Moreover, he may well arrive at this happy state much earlier than they do. This wider range, greater freedom and earlier satisfaction certainly do count for a lot to the topical/thematic collectors. In other words, they get their collecting fun more easily and earlier than the rest of the collectors.

In order to give the reader a useful focus, let's see how the other types of collecting—stamps, postal history and aerophilately—compare in the matter of freedom, fun and pleasure. Besides setting the thematic/topical scene, this exercise will also give the beginner some inkling of the relative advantages and disadvantages of these three other branches of collecting.

When collecting the stamps of one country, even in the case of the very large ones such as the USA or Great Britain, the day invariably comes when, for one reason or another, signs begin to appear that sooner or later this area of collecting will dry up. Of course, exploring the edges can be resorted to but this carries the risk of the comment that 'they don't belong' or some other similar remark. To escape from the restriction, the collector must either start on one of the other branches of collecting, such as postal history or aerophilately, or completely abandon the collection in favour of a new country. But both of these actions can easily result in some kind of setback and this means a waste of time, money and pleasure. Next it is interesting to notice the effect of two important points. The first is that the earlier issues of the 'better' countries are either very expensive or difficult to secure in a reasonable collecting condition. Then there is a kind of rejection effect which arises from the application of status differences between the expensive early stamps and the relatively inexpensive current issues. Thus the owner of a fine classical collection may well prefer not to buy the new issues whilst, at the other end of the scale, the collector of modern stamps avers that the high prices of the expensive early items result from nothing more than a market racket. The combined effect of these two influences is to produce a severe restriction which the one-country collector must endure. This is a restraint on his freedom and hence on his fun and pleasure.

On the other hand, the one-country stamp collector certainly enjoys a substantial bonus in the shape of the many collectable varieties, essays, proofs and specimens, all of which are still available to him. That is, of course, if he can afford today's spiralling prices. It is in his favour too that the thematic/topical collector can make use of many of these special items only in a rather limited number of cases. But, when he does use them, they are most valuable to his collecting.

Experience shows, on balance, it is now well established that it is the topical/thematic collector who enjoys the greater collecting freedom and pleasure.

Similarly, the postal-history collector has a very practical advantage in that he can start his collection right back in the fourteenth or fifteenth century, gathering much valuable and interesting material all the way up to the end of the twentieth century. But after about 1900 or thereabouts, the matter is quite different and many postal historians have no liking at all for modern material. Further, the postal-history collectors seem to hanker after the early and more expensive items, finding their attractions difficult to resist. The net effect is, as usually happens, that much of the very desirable postal-history material is priced well out of the reach of all but the most wealthy collectors.

Notice too another characteristic of the postal history collector. Very often he likes to dig deeply into his subject rather than range widely over it. Seeking out early and obscure details appears to be the proper thing to do. So the real area of his collecting freedom contracts more and more as his interest and enthusiasm grows. Finally, he grinds to a halt, finding himself not at all pleased with his collecting progress. In other words, he experiences unpleasure. Another result of these characteristics is that his collecting costs him more in time and cash than he at first envisaged and both are expensive these days. On the benefit side, of course, is the fact that he is concerned with a lively, rising market and his collection will most likely show a good cash profit if disposed of. But to most collectors that's for in the future and, at best, no more than paper profit. It's certainly not a pleasurable commodity.

The other area of collecting, aerophilately, is currently attracting quite a lot of attention. Here the collector must apply a relatively stringent test before he can justify the inclusion of an item in his collection. It is essential that the cover, card, etc., has in fact been flown, was intended for flight or was related to the organisation of a flight in some way. Sometimes there is an additional factor in that it is essential that a public service angle of some kind was involved. If an item does not satisfy at least one of these conditions it does not qualify for inclusion in the collection. As a result, many of the most interesting areas of collecting relating to the arts, culture and the rest of the humanities are largely denied to the aerophilatelist.

On the credit side, he certainly enjoys a wide and attractive freedom in that his collecting may well range over many countries and peoples. Also, if he can brave a little criticism, he can include in his collection many items which, although only weakly connected to an actual flight, do fall in the peripheral areas.

The aerophilatelist also often encounters another serious limitation. After about 1920 the plethora of first flights which took place has produced the idea that nothing after that date is of any real aerophilatelic value. This is especially so in the competitive world. There are also strong signs that although aerophilately is a comparatively new form of collecting, the effects of market forces and of scarcity have already pushed many desirable items well out of reach of many collectors. There are, then, in this area of collecting as in postal history, a number of restricting conditions which impose real and severe limitations on both the range and the pleasure of his collecting activities.

Now let's turn to the thematic/topical collector. On the credit side the freedom he enjoys to draw his material from any philatelic area he chooses is so evident that the other collectors are becoming increasingly envious of him. There is no country, period or angle of thinking in which he may not hopefully and fruitfully search for collectable material. But, a word of caution! This happy freedom is in no sense an absolute one because there is an overall condition which applies to all the types of thematic collection: all the items in the collection must be clearly relevant to the theme or subject. This is important both for the collector and the would-be collector and more on this follows later in the book.

In fairness, there are some other restrictions which come into play in this type of collecting; they are both practical and personal. Their nature and extent will be covered in the chapters which follow. But, because they are much smaller in effect than those imposed on the stamp collector, the postal historian and the aerophilatelist, and also because they fall within a vastly wider scope of collecting activity, they are far more easily taken care of by the topical/thematic collector.

Whilst considering the relative advantages and disadvantages of this type of collecting over the others, there is one factor which certainly cannot be overlooked. The process of selecting one or two items out of a very wide range of material undoubtedly results in the thematist having an extremely interesting collection. It has variety in abundance. But alongside this there is very often a considerable quantity of broken ranges of stamps which cannot be put to use. Such material has little or no market value and it can only be put into a saleable condition by robbing the collection and so completing the full set. But the future is not quite as black as it looks at present. Already a number of dealers are prepared to supply stamps against topical wants lists and as the popularity of thematics/topicals grows this market will improve.

Then just where does the topical/thematic collector stand in this matter of balance between advantages and disadvantages? Over samples taken in Great Britain, America and Europe there is no doubt that on the whole there are more happy and well-satisfied collectors in thematics than in any other branch of philately.

The dimensions of freedom

It is a little unwise to lightheartedly suppose, as so many do, that the thematic/topical enthusiast may draw the material for his collection equally well from any source he wishes and achieve a totally satisfying result. At best this idea is very much theoretical. This book is essentially practical and it is therefore vital that the reader should get the correct picture of the real dimension of this thematic freedom without delay. So what is the true extent of this wider range, this greater freedom, which is so valuable and so enjoyable?

The major factor governing the true range or extent of a collection is, of course, the total number of stamps, covers and the like items existing, which are relevant to any particular theme, subject or topic. In this connection, it is useful to note that the difference between the amount of relevant material which can be found varies very greatly from one title to another. This wide difference can have a very considerable effect on the size and hence the cost of the collection. It also governs the complexity or otherwise which the collector must find to his liking. The author suggests, without restricting the freedom of the reader in any way whatsoever, that there may well be some merit in considering the practical aspect of thematic/topical freedom. Here are two examples illustrating the extent to which the choice of subject governs the amount of real freedom which you will enjoy during the collecting.

Firstly, if you choose the simple title of 'Ships' as the subject of your collection—possibly because it will be so very easy to collect (and this is not synonymous with collecting freedom)—what then is the true freedom picture for you? Well, there are in excess of 25,000 stamps with a ship of some sort on them. At ten stamps to a page this means you must buy about 2,600 album pages, find all those stamps, mount and house them. That's going to call for around 50 albums full and a good long life's work. Over and above this, there are a vast number of covers, postal markings, slogans and the like, all of which justify a place in the collection. But before going further, let's get nearer the practicalities of this collection, shall we? On very many of the stamps the ship will be seen as no more than an insignificant feature and merely a little piece of artistic decoration. To include these would be indulging in purposeless collecting. That's just what topicals/thematics is not! Even if the ship is of reasonable size it may still not be possible to identify its type, the part of the world it would be used in, let alone the actual name of the vessel. Some collectors, because they cannot attach a story to the ship, regard the stamp as only relevant to the subject in a secondary sort of way. Others, happily say 'That ship is a ship' and include it in or out just as they personally prefer. Nor do they need a reason for whichever line they take. So what is the effect of discriminating about relevancy? Our total of 26,000 stamps might well be reduced to about 7,000. Adding in sufficient covers, markings and slogans etc. to make the collection attractive, might well produce a massive holding of some 25 albums. To fill them will need a considerable amount of time and money of course. But your pleasure and enjoyment will have been sustained over many years; your stock of fun seemingly unending.

Now let's look at the other end of the scale. A collection with the title 'Meteorology' might show about 500 stamps and materially less than 100 other items, and all of these could be nicely housed in two or three albums with a little space to spare. So the total cost and space required for the collection is vastly less than for the 'Ship' collection mentioned previously. But the amount of pleasure and happy interest produced by the 'Meteorology' collection could be at least as great as that enjoyed by the owner of the 'Ship' collection. Of course, the nature of their enjoyments will differ. And that, too, is what collecting is all about.

Collectors are happy people. Their pleasure and fun come first in all circumstances. Sometimes, of course, as with human nature, they have second thoughts. Very often these result from an appreciation of the real dimensions of thematic/topical freedom.

Explanations, definitions and examples
The words 'theme' and 'topical' have many applications in everyday life, ranging from the commonplace to the unusual and the erudite. Despite all of these, as collectors we are fully entitled to enjoy the freedom of placing our own interpretations on what is meant to us by these two words. Moreover, having

our own ideas about them, we should both recognise and respect what others think because they are doing no more than exercising one of many rights of collectors in general. That's what the freedom of collecting is all about!

Philatelic organisations must have workable rules and, therefore, produce definitions (of 'topical' and 'theme') to meet their own requirements. So, in turn these too should be equally well recognised and respected. The fact that there are sometimes substantial differences between the definitions adopted by one group of collectors or organisations need not be the least bit disturbing because, in essence, each is attempting to cater for the special outlook of only a part of the collecting world.

The generic terms 'thematic' and 'topical' when used in collecting have quite broadly based applications and understandings. The reader will find definitions and explanations of them as generally understood in Great Britain and America, in the next paragraph. Although certain differences may be noted between them, these are mainly a matter of terminology and the real impact on the collector need only be quite small. Despite this, some collectors frequently make much more of these differences than is justified.

Here it is! The total field of topical/thematic collecting is made up of two components or branches. These are, in Great Britain and Europe: thematic collections and subject collections; in the Americas: thematic collections and topical collections.

It must be remarked, however, that largely as a matter of convenience collectors both in America and Great Britain very often use the terms 'thematic' and 'topical' quite loosely to describe any of the types of collection listed above. The author wishes to make it clear that collectors are perfectly free to recognise these divisions or not, just as they please. Those in the non-competitive area of collecting in fact have not the slightest need to do so. But the rules of the organised philatelic bodies, especially those concerned with exhibitions and competitions, do frequently call for a certain degree of recognition of these or similar divisions.

The author suggests that there is little purpose in worrying about the fact that the two basic words 'thematic' and 'topical' are in common use as the title for a particular sort of collection. Here is the picture again.

It is of further interest, especially in the world of competitive collecting, to note that further divisions are recognised. These are much more a matter of historical rather than contemporary use and detailed information about them will be found in the Appendix Part F.

The theme collection
Let's start with a rather long but very useful definition:

A theme collection is one which, starting from the subject on the stamp, the postal or philatelic document or item is assembled to a set plan and develops logically some particular theme or illustrates an idea or presents a thesis.

Notice here that a theme collection can develop along any of three lines: a particular theme; or to illustrate an idea; or to present a thesis. These three types are very interesting but also very important because they give the clues as to the basic ideas contained within the term 'theme'. Here, very briefly, are examples of each of these three types.

A PARTICULAR THEME
A collection carrying the title 'Oil in the Service of Man' could be effectively planned to show where and how oil was first discovered and the immediate effects which resulted. This could be followed by stamps showing how it is now obtained, refined and distributed. To show the many and wide fields of use on land, sea and air, however, would call for a considerable amount of space, care and thought to bring out nicely the service enjoyed by mankind. This collection could then be developed to cover the many by-products of oil, their manufacture and uses. Besides the benefits of oil, the collection

could bring out some other factors such as pollution, energy conservation and war.

ILLUSTRATING AN IDEA

Under the title 'The Activities of the Police Force' the collection could be arranged to suggest the idea that the man in the street does not fully appreciate the many roles of the police. The assemblage of stamps and philatelic items could start with the unpleasant conditions which existed before the establishment of the police force, its introduction and growth. The bulk of the collection would be devoted to the many and varied ways in which the police are required to carry out their duties. Here the idea behind the collection seems to be to say 'Look at these stamps, doesn't it surprise you that the police are called upon to work in such a wide field for your benefit?'

PRESENTING A THESIS (I.E. PUTTING A PROPOSITION OR AN AFFIRMATION)

By the careful selection and presentation of stamps, documents and covers, the collector could pose a question as wide as, for example, 'Scientific Growth, Good or Bad?'. Thus the collection could be developed to show the growth of science in medicine, transport, communications, leisure and easy living, adding man's increasing longevity for good measure. On the other hand further stamps could be arranged to show that the growth of science has been accompanied by real losses in the arts, culture and of literary ability. Add the effects of war, famine, erosion and the innumerable technical failures which have occurred and the collector could easily wonder whether scientific growth had proved to be more for our destruction than for our good. Alternatively, the emphasis could be turned in the other and more happy direction.

Each of the three types described, if it is to be effective and to present its ideas satisfactorily, within the theme definition needs to be logically developed. To these ends, therefore, a certain amount of planning is required before beginning to assemble the collection proper. The material for the collection must be located and bought before it can be put to use in the collection. This means nothing less than ensuring that the planning must be started, constructed, and in firm shape (in so far as the experience of the collector allows) before the start of buying. This makes planning a basic activity and a considerable amount of space is, therefore, given in the book to collection planning.

The subject collection

The definition of a subject collection states that it comprises all of the stamps, philatelic documents and other items which have a bearing on: the illustrative subject concerned; or the purpose for which the stamps were issued. Please note that this definition is intended to draw the reader's attention to the two types of collection within the common title of subject.

EXAMPLES OF SUBJECT COLLECTIONS

These can have quite simple titles such as 'Birds', 'Flowers', 'Ships', 'Music' or 'Buildings'. But the use of a simple, easy title does not necessarily infer that the collection is correspondingly simple and easy. Indeed there are many subject collections which are not only extensive and excellently planned, but also call for a very detailed and expert knowledge of the subject in question.

The primary requirement of a subject collection is that the stamps and other items should be selected to show a good, clear picture of the subject proper, i.e. it must be portrayed on the stamp.

The example given here of a subject collection might apply equally well to flowers or birds. The easiest way to show these is to place them in the alphabetical order of the country of issue and in date order within each group. This sort of collection has pictorial merit because it shows all the kinds of flowers (or birds) likely to be found in each area in the fashion of a panorama. A rather more particular way of arranging the collection might be to disregard completely the country and date of issue and to show the subjects in strictly botanical order for the flower collection (or species in the bird collection). Such arrangements certainly require the collector to have a very good knowledge of botany in the first example, and ornithology in the second. Surprisingly enough, there are a large number of collections set up on a scientific basis in the stamp world. Stamps which show the subject or have a direct bearing on it by accident rather than by design are, of course, proper to the collection. For example, one of the stamps of the Bahamas shows a flamingo in flight, so it could, therefore, find a good place in a collection of birds on stamps. However, it was designed as an airmail stamp but the projected route failed to materialise and so the stamps, being very attractive, were called into general use instead.

THE FURTHER DIVISIONS OF THE SUBJECT GROUP OF COLLECTIONS
Compared with traditional stamp collecting, topical/thematic collecting is still young. Shortly after the start of thematics and when the competitive angle emerged, it was thought essential that it should be divided into three equally important parts. These were (a) theme, (b) subject and (c) purpose of issue. This arrangement required the use of three distinct sets of judging criteria and standards of marks. There was an emphasis on originality and very often the line of distinction between a subject and a purpose of issue entry was not clear. After some years it was appreciated that some degree of simplification was essential. Both the international (FIP) and the Inter-American organisations finally adopted a two division set-up. These are the thematic and the subject classes, with the latter containing both the former subject and purpose of issue collections. Here is the complete and current picture.

Both the subject collections of Great Britain and the topical collections of the Americas have two subdivisions, thus:

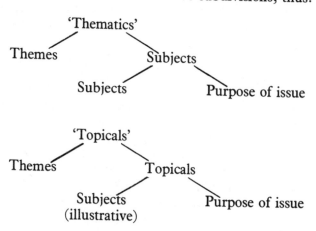

You may well be tempted to ask the most reasonable question 'Why bother at all about these subdivisions?' The short answer is 'You personally need not unless you wish.' Recognising them, however, may well make talking to other collectors so much more easy, so much more pleasurable. Why not?

The purpose of issue collection

This is an arrangement of all of the stamps and other items which have been issued, bearing in mind a purpose rather than a subject. Thus for example, 'Freedom from Hunger' is an international purpose for which many countries have repeatedly issued one or two stamps as a set. Similarly, the lives and works of Shakespeare and of Copernicus were made the reason for the issue of sets of commemorative stamps and miniature sheets. Note that all the stamps issued for these purposes are proper to the collection irrespective of whether the main item—i.e. Shakespeare or Copernicus—is actually portrayed. Other sets may show such aspects as a birthplace, seat of learning, as well as places important in the works or life.

The line between theme and subject collecting

In the world of collecting, freedom to develop the collection in just the way you particularly prefer is by far the most satisfying. In these circumstances there can be no hard and fast line between the theme and the subject areas. Nor is there the slightest need to make the fact that distinctions have been made as between one type of collection and another the be all and end all of your collecting life.

Thus a collection could well be started with a strong subject characteristic but later, possibly after the owner has benefited from an inspiration, develop into a well-defined theme. As an example of this, a suggestion was made to an acquaintance that he might well 'do' medicine as an interesting subject. At that point in time it certainly seemed that such a collection showing the many kinds, origins and uses of medicine would fit his bill very nicely. A couple of years later, although he had a good showing of the ideas which we had talked over, there was much in evidence in the collection of a well-developed theme of 'For the Sick, Medicine'. Happily he explained that the subject which he started with was very interesting but it had no humanity about it. This was the angle which really did appeal to him. One glance at the section of his theme on tropical medicine and mankind convinced me how right he was to allow his personal interest, and not the 'rules and regulations' to direct his collecting activities. Wisely enough he agreed that it would be quite disastrous to mix the two styles in his competitive efforts. The criterion is, of course, the yield-out of fun and pleasure which the collecting affords.

Pleasure needs to be planned

Pleasure and satisfaction are very personal experiences and all collectors are fully entitled to their share. Many collectors do manage to enjoy the fullest participation but, alas, there are some who do not always have such happy experiences. It seems that, soon after the start of collecting, an element of unease creeps in. Then this may degenerate into disquiet and finally disillusionment. Although this book is not concerned with the psychology of collecting but with getting satisfaction from it, this matter cannot, in fairness, be left entirely with the reader. The author, therefore, takes the liberty of suggesting that one of the best possible insurances against such unhappy results is to plan both before and during collecting activities. But do not make hard labour of it, but try to remember that if no plan whatsoever is formulated at the start of collecting you may well run certain risks. So, let there be a plan!

Topical/thematic expertise

The interest and enjoyment which you can derive from your collection mainly depends on your thematic capability. This might well be termed your 'thematic expertise'. Now experience shows that expertise of this sort is made up of quite a number of related components and the effects of some of these can have quite decisive effects both on the progress made and the results achieved.

Please do not assume that all this adds up to a lot of rules and regulations because it does not! It amounts to no more than taking a common-sense view well before the start of buying even the album sheets, of what to collect and how to do it. That's it: what to collect and how to do it!

THE IMPORTANT COMPONENTS OF EXPERTISE

A separate chapter is devoted to each of the most important components which make up topical/thematic expertise. These are:

1   Theme and subject (or topic) selection
2   Starting the collection
3   Collecting methods
4   Presentation

In practice these are not entirely separate aspects of collecting but overlap at certain points. Your personal expertise will, however, easily provide the link between them. This linkage, being a personal one, will allow you to make each of them just as important (and, therefore, pleasant) as you prefer. Thus some collectors find that the niceties of good, clean presentation are secondary to the enjoyment of finding and mounting the stamps and other philatelic items. To others there is special pleasure in seeing their album sheets well set up, nicely balanced and in ship-shape order.

Irrespective of which angles you find the more enjoyable, the four components given earlier remain the bedrock of your collecting capability and, as such, they fully deserve all the care and attention which you can possibly give to them.

1　First Thoughts

The uses of the collection

Although this book is essentially practical it also contains a considerable number of collecting angles which are somewhat theoretical. So the reader's focus is moved between the purely mechanical aspects of collecting on the one hand and the highly personal on the other. Both of these, of course, make a material contribution to the success, satisfaction and pleasure of collecting. In this way it is hoped that the collector, and the would-be collectors, will avoid suffering such disconcerting thoughts as 'Later on, I discovered that . . .' or 'Too late I realised that. . . .' Over the years the author has heard such expressions many times indeed.

One of the purposes of this wide-angle coverage is to allow the collector (a) to appreciate that the style in which the collection is put together has a very strong bearing on the uses which it has to him; (b) to settle in his own mind, and in the light of (a), the lines on which the collection is to be arranged.

This interconnection of the two facets—how the collection is formed and the uses to be made of it—will exist throughout the progress of collecting. It is relevant therefore to ask about the methods and objects of the collections.

In topical/thematic collecting certain factors and disciplines can be recognised. These differ according to how the collection is to be used—for purely personal enjoyment or in exhibitions and competitions.

Please note that this division into non-competitive and competitive collections is made here purely to help the nice understanding of the nature of the world of collecting as it exists today. There are, of course, no such clear divisions of collectors, no clubs or societies catering for competitive rather than non-competitive collectors, or vice versa. The distinction is seen in the collections themselves and what is done with them. Very often a collector is in both camps—and why not? Isn't freedom in collecting the paramount and only real objective?

Non-competitive collecting

Many collectors have not the slightest desire to enter any sort of competition. The sheets of their collection are arranged in the way that pleases them most and they are free to change this if and when they so desire. It is of not the slightest concern to them whether or not their style or material is suitable for the competitive world. The author considers, as do many others, that they are as good collectors as competition devotees with an equal place in the world of topical/thematic collecting.

But it is not to be supposed that they are entirely free from limitation. True, they do not have to observe the regulations made by others; nevertheless they invariably find themselves conforming to a code of 'rules' which, unknowingly, they have constructed for themselves. They think and often say 'To my way of thinking, it's best done like this . . .' or 'I like it done this way. . . .' These are expressions of the basic freedoms of collectors and we should try to recognise and respect them accordingly. They are good, sound thematic/topical collectors in every sense of the word.

On the other side of the picture, the competitive collector has a much clearer goal in mind, and whether he achieves it or not is frequently unimportant. He must observe not only the rules of the competition but also seek to understand them through the eyes of the organisers and judges. If success is to be achieved he must discipline himself to follow all the requirements and not overlook some. However, he will be the type of collector who thoroughly enjoys most such disciplines. It is part of his particular collecting pleasure to fix his intentions on a certain standard in the competition and then work undauntedly to reach it. To have an object in mind is his spur; to concentrate his search for just the right type of material and then to find it, are no small part of his fun. Equally pleasing to him are his nicely presented sheets and the carefully selected stamps and covers. The prospectus and catalogue of the exhibition are important items for him and the anticipation of a good award this time, or perhaps next, is a very real part of his personal satisfaction.

But the competitor's life is not just roses, roses all the way! Sometimes, when the results of the competition are announced, his high hopes get an unhappy jolt. Maybe it will take several months to recover from the shock and regain the former enthusiasm. But this is the same as in many other walks of life—the rough must be taken with the smooth.

Irrespective of whether he wins or not, the competitive collector is an enthusiast, an excellent topical/thematic technician who believes in collecting with an object and enjoys the excitements. So, he too is a good collector.

On new ground

The experiences of nearly all the well-established thematic/topical collectors reveal the fact that there are often benefits to be gained by having some knowledge of traditional stamp collecting. Further, in non-competitive collecting the amount needed for excellent and absorbing results is almost minimal. In the competitive world, however, it is recognised that to gain even a fair award it is essential to have a good working knowledge of philately, especially at international levels.

Generally speaking, as much knowledge is needed as the subject demands, its use requires and you find necessary for your enjoyment. With the help of some knowledge of stamps your collecting life will be easier. The collection will take shape better (but possibly not earlier) and the sum total of pleasure becomes greater. Further, it is a considerable benefit to be tuned in to the whole world of stamp collecting, its literature, its collectors and their collections.

If you are beginning on entirely new ground—making a start in both stamps and thematics—you have two jobs to tackle in earnest. The twin processes of acquiring philatelic knowledge and thematic capability require you to be on two parallel courses. Despite the fact that you can sail your collecting boats only one at a time, achieving both objectives is by no means so difficult as it seems. Here are two ways to do it and you can choose (with or without modifications as you wish) so as best to suit your personal requirements. Here they are:

1   To become a stamp collector first and a topical/thematic collector next. This is the ideal method but it is both time- and interest-consuming. If you have that amount of time to devote to the exercise and can stay the course (this might last a couple of years) your philatelic and thematic capability should eventually be above criticism. So, unless your sights are set very high indeed, try the following alternative:

2   The second course of action is practical even for the would-be enthusiast who can spare only limited time and interest for this double job. It is based on starting the two processes of acquiring philatelic knowledge and commencing collecting at roughly the same time and allowing them to grow in parallel. In the early stages, more time and thought must be given to the basics of stamp-collecting terminology and practice even if this is at the expense of your thematic activity. The merit of starting with the philatelic side first is that it ensures that you get the fundamentals of stamp collecting before becoming too enthusiastically involved in the topical/thematic aspect. The author suggests that, the more sound your grounding in philately, the more benefit you will reap. Thereafter try to work into the two areas, stamps and thematics, turn and turn about.

Doubtless the question you will now ask is something like 'So far so good, but exactly how long, for me in particular, is a limited amount of time?' Rates of gaining know-how vary widely and it is therefore not possible to give even a very rough estimate of the time needed. You can, however, get a reasonable answer to the question for yourself with the aid of the three groups of items which follow. The total range of these covers nearly the whole field of philatelic expertise.

The first, Group 1, should be considered as a minimal requirement. It has two parts: (a) practical work; and (b) basic terms. These will acquaint you with elementary stamp-collecting practice and certain philatelic terms. Even with this minimum you can set up a very good straightforward topical/thematic collection. But here's a thought. It ought not to be supposed that the knack of mounting stamps and handling items will 'come to you automatically' without taking steps to acquire it.

The second group (Group 2) takes far longer. In return it will pay a dividend by equipping you with a very good grounding in the many philatelic terms in use today.

The last (Group 3) covers most of the finer points of stamp collecting and will give you the opportunity to become even more knowledgeable.

Now for how best to use these three groups. First, look over all the items carefully. Do not worry if some have little or no meaning for you at present. Try to relate them to what you know or can do easily and happily at this point. The following notes will help you decide your course of action.

Right at the start you will see that a few of the terms are followed by 'AM'. These are in common use in America but may well be quite new to the collectors of Great Britain and Europe. Their meanings are given in the Appendix page 37.

Information on both the practical side and the meaning of the terms given can be obtained from the books listed in the Bibliography.

If you decide to go the whole hog, to give yourself the chance of getting in the top flight, the total of Groups 1, 2 and 3 is your objective. And that's quite a lot both to do and to think about.

On the other hand, if you are quite new to collecting, your line must be very different. Here is a suggestion. Plan to complete all Group 1 before you begin to do any collecting proper, even if it requires some effort. Why? Because at this stage even a modest amount of collecting enthusiasm can run away with you. When you have had a fair taste of the first pleasures of collecting, then work your way through Group 2. Do this in steps, according to your convenience, and break these up with further spells of collecting. In this way you ensure that your pleasure and fun grows, not dulled by the task of getting the philatelic know-how. Make the excercise a two-sided way of enjoying yourself by doing just enough of the philately and the collecting in turn to keep you happy. Of course, if you are a well-established stamp collector, with a fair working knowledge of the majority of the items in Groups 1 and 2, your life will be a lot easier. Why not make it more enjoyable? So, after checking up on your real capability in respect of the first two groups, browse over the items in Group 3. You may be intrigued enough by some of them to go exploring for more fun and relaxation. You can afford it! Here are the three groups:

Group 1:

A   Securing practical capability in:

(a) *Stamps*
handling
separation
storage
application of mounts (hinges)
mounting on album sheets
removal of old hinges
removal from paper

(b) *Albums and sheets, selection*
types of sheet
advantages and disadvantages
album types
costs

(c) *Sheets, best (preferred) method of:*
laying out sheets with stamps
laying out sheets with covers and stamps
writing up
storage

(d) *Miscellaneous*
use of mounting corners
use of mounting aids
use of perforation gauge
watermark detection

(e) *Understanding how to read catalogues*

B   Knowing the meaning of:

definitive	precancelled
commemorative	cancellation
semi-postal (AM)	handstamp
mint	cachet (see *Illustration 1.1*)
used	cachet (AM)
perforation	CTO
imperforate	pre-adhesive
sheet	entire

pane	handback (AM)
gutter	
margin	bordered papers (AM)
selvage (AM)	
phosphor	surcharge
tagging (AM)	overprint
zip (AM)	duplicate
plate block	
control	non-profit (AM)
error (AM)	certified (AM)
freak (AM)	
	airletter
	postal stationery
	postcard
	postal card

Note: The following terms are dealt with after Group 3: maximum cards, miniature sheets, postal history items, aerophilatelic; the terms marked with '(AM)' American are explained in the Appendix to this chapter.

Group 2:

A   Skills

obtaining balance on sheets
backing items
identifying water marks

B   Knowing the meaning of:

airgram	private post
backprint	research
bisect	research (AM)
black blot	se–tenant
chalk-surfaced paper	ship letter
essay	special delivery
fiscal	specimen
forbidden issue	tabs
jubilee line	tête bêche
obliteration	tied
packet letter	undesirable issue
parcel stamp	

Group 3:

A   Skills
justification
identifying types of paper

B   Terms

colour trial	phantom
comb perforation	photogravure
die proof	plate proof
forgery	re-entry
imprimatur	retouch
interpanneau margins	reprint
line engraved	roulette
line perforation	surface printed
officials	TPO

More about some collecting items

There are certain items which, although very popular and very useful to the topical/thematic collector, deserve rather more thought from the discerning enthusiast. The following are given here a more careful consideration than appears in the usual dictionary of philatelic terms or glossary. They are:

1   Maximum cards
2   Miniature sheets
3   Postal-history items
4   Aerophilatelic items

1   MAXIMUM CARDS

Maximum cards are picture postcards depicting the subject of a postage stamp and which have the same stamp affixed on the picture side and are cancelled on the first day of the stamp or the anniversary date. This cancellation may be official or privately sponsored.

There are several points to be made in connection with the use of the maximum card in Great Britain. The British Post Office requires that the illustration on the card should bear some relationship to the new issue of a stamp, and that it is dealt with as a first day issue. Next, a postmark which will satisfy collectors—clear and legible regarding the point of posting and the date—cannot always be given on highly glossy cards, because the ink does not penetrate the surface and smudges easily. Further, the stamp may become detached in transit because of the high gloss and this makes the card of little use to the collector.

Generally the maximum card occupies a large proportion of an album page. If it is responsible for any overcrowding, or destroys the balance or appearance of the page, it is really of negative value. A maximum card which is well produced and shows the subject in clear and faithful detail improves the artistic merit of the collection. One which adds clarity and detail to the stamp and is also finely produced benefits the collection both thematically and artistically. The extent to which maximum cards may be suitably used in collections is covered further in Chapters 2 and 3.

2 MINIATURE SHEETS

First they are not a miniature as regards size of the stamp but have a miniature resemblance to a stamp pane or sheet. But this similarity is only partial and since their introduction the attractiveness has been increased by ornamentation, changes in shape and size as well as the inclusion of non-postal elements. They consist essentially of either one stamp of an issue printed on a larger sheet or of all those issued at a specific date, printed together on one sheet. Special designs may be inserted between the stamps, which can be perforated as in the normal stamp or imperforate. Miniature sheets are produced on a special piece of paper with a surround which usually bears a legend and carries a design. As a postal item they carry only the status of the appropriate issuing body. With postal validity they can be used on first day covers but the overlarge-sized cover needed makes them difficult to include in the collection.

In certain circumstances the miniature sheet can make a positive contribution to the progress of the collection. But some official miniature sheets are no more than a straight multiple of the issued stamp(s) and can never, therefore, do any more thematically than the stamp proper.

Colour illustration 1 shows a miniature sheet with each stamp the same but having a special pictorial border. In the theme 'The Tree and Mankind' this border shows the several stages of the tree from planting to cutting, and thence to the use of the resulting timber. It is therefore of substantial value to this theme. On the other hand, the Ceylon miniature sheet from 'Birds' *(Colour illustration 2)* is highly artistic and would make an attractive item in a non-competitive collection. From the point of view of the subject, however, the drawings of the birds shown on the very extensive border give very little more than is shown on the stamps. In other words, this sheet does very little to advance the subject and its use in a competitive entry accordingly adds little merit. Although a miniature sheet may fit excellently into the theme/subject, it should be recognised that sometimes the circumstances in which it was issued were ethically unsatisfactory. Its use, therefore, especially ,in competitive thematics, should be carefully considered. There is more about this later.

Souvenir sheets
These are small printed sheets showing some event or stamp germane to the purpose of the exhibition at which they are sold. Not all have postal validity but they are usually excellently printed and, therefore, attractive items. Because they are often available only at the particular exhibition or thereafter, via a dealer in stamps, it is noticeable that their cost has shown a tendency to increase very rapidly when the event closes. Many, therefore, rank as collectors' items of value. In non-competitive thematic collecting, the questions of postal validity and space utilisation are of secondary importance. The only requirement is that they should be well and truly relative to the theme/subject. In competitive thematics, very much greater care is needed before including the miniature sheet in the entry and expecting it to attract merit.

3   POSTAL-HISTORY ITEMS
Postal history includes the way letters were carried from the earliest times up to now, together with the handstamps on them, the organisation of the posts, and the changes therein. Generally a detailed study of the adhesive postage stamp is not recognised as postal history. Any item which a postal historian uses, providing it is relative to the theme/subject of the thematist is proper for him also. The test is then 'Is this item

relative to my topic, subject or theme?' If so it can be included safely and to advantage in the thematic collection. To show an item so selected and its use, the reader should look at *Illustration 1.2*, which was used in a collection exhibited under the title of 'The Watchers of the Skies'. The inclusion was considered to be creditable. By allowing the inclusion of an astronomical event for which no stamps were issued, it introduced an element of variety into the exhibit and the cover is unusual and not at all easy to find. Items like this add to the attractiveness and value of the collection and opportunity should be taken to secure them wherever possible.

Exhibits and talks on postal history are fair fields for ideas about suitable items for the collection. A word of warning here. However attractive the item or reasonable the price, if it is not, in all truth, clearly relevant to the theme, topic or subject, it ought not to be included in the collection.

4   AEROPHILATELIC ITEMS

Nearly all aerophilatelic material is related to the postal history of flight in some form, i.e. covers (that is envelopes) which have been or were intended for carriage in flight. All such items, when relative to the subject, are good for collecting. Also in this category are the special stamps or overprints on stamps authorised for particular flights. Aerophilatelists, however, make use of maps, documents and other non-postal material to help explain or support the story which their sheets tell. Such material is fine for the aerophilatelist and for the non-competitive thematic collector. For the competitor there are two points which should be taken into account. These are (a) that the conditions of some exhibitions and competitions specifically bar this type of material; and (b) care must be taken that the non-aerophilatelic item does not overpower the stamps and other postal items. The question should be asked 'Is the large amount of space which the cover etc. will occupy fully justified or could it be put to better use?'

Survival rate and outlook

On reading the above you may well say 'What an extraordinary thing to have in a book about topicals and thematics—survival rate?' The author suggests that you should contain your surprise until having read this section. Maybe it will be of greater interest and value than you supposed. It can pay off too.

Comments: 'I could see this one [theme] getting out of hand' or 'That one [topical] faded out on me'. Expressions such as these are not infrequently heard when talking to collectors. From their tones it is only too apparent that these are not the best or happiest of times for them. Sometimes the remarks are accompanied by clear evidence of regret and disappointments at what has been 'inflicted' upon them. But if this should happen more than once to a collector the loss of interest is so great that collecting is no longer a pleasureable activity. Then the loss of time and money is felt with regret, the whole exercise becomes unpalatable and the end of collecting is now well in sight. This is not an emotional but a realistic picture.

Are you set on a course of collecting of this sort? Or, are your plans, seemingly sound enough at the moment, likely to get you inescapably into such an unhappy position? If you are about to start collecting, do you want to experience an inevitable fade-out? Perhaps there is something to be said for thinking about the survival prospects of your topic, theme or subject and for doing this, if you can, well before a start is made. Let's see if this seemingly odd subject can be put into suitable focus, shall we?

Firstly, it is certainly not a failure if stopping collecting or the slowing down of activity is for good and sound reasons, even if there are tears and regrets. It is the reasons for the slow-down or the halt that matter. Here are some of the more usual.

The first and one of the more frequent reasons for fade-out is that the collector chooses a topic, theme or subject for which he has no real liking or knowledge. When the crunch comes the thought is 'However did I get myself into this subject?' Perhaps an attractive article appeared on the pleasures of collecting this or that. It stirs you a bit and is well written too. Or perhaps you see a bright set of stamps on what at first sight seems to be a good long-running project. But is this topic really for you? You should ask yourself a few simple questions such as: 'Have I a real liking for this subject? Was that article so attractive because of the subject appeal or because it was nicely written and well illustrated?' Certainly do not miss the critical question, 'What do I know about the background to this theme, let alone some of the details?' The answers to questions of this type, before you are committed to the project, may well help you make a reasonable estimate of the survival prospects ahead.

Now for another likely reason. Has the proposed subject a sufficiently large stamp content to allow a reasonably satisfactory collection to be set up without the need to scour the ends of the earth for material? Such subjects can and do occur in the usual way of casting around for a bright and attractive area of collecting. To think that this question can be easily answered by dipping into a stamp catalogue is unsatisfactory because it will take so long to do this effectively. It may produce results which allow no decision to be taken, and then you are no further ahead. Tackling this problem is returned to in Chapter 6. But again the point is highlighted that there is a need to consider survival prospects when seeking a suitable subject.

On the other hand, the choice of an over-wide topic or subject may well make you vulnerable. There are many examples to be found—ships, children on stamps and the like, to name but a few. Choosing a wide-based subject is fine and easy but the mistake occurs when you fail to discriminate sufficiently as to which stamps or section of the subject should be included in the collection. This too is explored in the next chapter.

Briefly then, there are sound reasons for the thought that the selection of the right subject, topic or theme can do much for your satisfaction and pleasure. You may well save time and money and avoid the possibility of the loss of pleasure and collecting fun. This matter of making a good choice is so important that a complete chapter in this book is devoted to it. The object is to ensure you have a positive picture, in the clearest possible terms, of how to choose your area of collecting.

Survival rate? Now it is certainly very much in your interest, is it not!

Appendix

A

The following terms are used in America but are not understood generally in Great Britain.

Collateral—Material used in a collection which, although

relevant to the theme/topical/subject is of a non-philatelic nature. Generally inadmissible in competitive thematics. *Colour illustration 3* shows an example of its use. The sales folder in the upper part of the sheet is very interesting but collateral.

Fun—Pleasure, enjoyment—but not sport, amusement, jocularity, drollery or fooling—in the collecting world.

Rate hike—A progressive increase in (postal) rates over a stated period.

Slated—Placed on record to occur, for example, 'A new issue of . . . is slated.' This means that the details of a new issue have been published. No criticism is implied.

B

The following are the accepted meanings in America for the terms marked (AM) in Group 1, Part B and Group 2, Part B.

Group 1, Part B

Bordered papers—Album sheets with a purpose-printed border and design. See *Colour illustration 6.*

Cachet—In America this term is most frequently used for the printed design or illustration on the left-hand side of a cover. In Great Britain the term cachet is used only of a special hand or machine mark applied to a cover to show a particular usage. Both the American and the British types of cachet are shown in *Illustration 1.1.*

Certified (mail)—Stamps issued to show that some form of certificate of postage is involved.

Error—A major mistake in the production of a stamp including imperforate, part perforation, missing and wrong colours, doubling and inversion.

Freak—An abnormal variety created by a unique set of circumstances, e.g. paper fold, perforation shift etc., as opposed to a continuously appearing variety or major error. See *Colour illustration 4* of a Bahamas overprint caused by the accidental folding of a corner of the stamp.

Handback—A letter cancelled by the Administration at a special point and immediately handed back to the owner and thus not transmitted by postal means to the recipient.

Non-profit (stamps)—Stamps issued for use by approved organisations not having a profit-intended object and allowed postage at reduced rates.

Selvage—The unprinted part of a sheet or pane margin (i.e. border).

Semi-postal—A stamp issued for the purpose of producing a contribution to a charitable cause as well as to defray postage.

Tagging—Phosphur markings applied to stamps to facilitate automatic sorting.

Zip—A sign placed in the margin of a sheet or pane of stamps to remind the senders of letters to add the postal or zip code to the address.

Group 2, Part B

Research—In Great Britain this term indicates study in depth to locate and check known information and conclusions, then discover new facts and postulate further conclusions. In America it generally refers to the location and extraction of details given in references other than catalogues. The author came to appreciate the difference in usage of this word whilst he was in America. Sitting over a cup of coffee at an exposition, he noted two ladies looking interestedly at some unsorted piles of bird and flower stamps. One of them remarked to the other, 'I shall have to research these . . .' to which the other lady replied 'You certainly must, I'll lend you my catalogues, of course'. Scenting an Anglo-American terminology difference, this little domestic scene was discussed with a number of American and British collectors. Two important points emerged. They are (1) that the non-competitive collector uses this term (research) freely and without very precise definition; (2) in the competitive area of collection much more care is needed. Thus the rules for international events require '*careful research by the collector allowing his personality to be brought forth*' for theme entries, and that '*deep philatelic research*' is needed for subject entries. If you intend to exhibit at an international, do try to keep these requirements well in mind. It is of note that one of the British national events (the BPE) includes '*personal research*' as a judging aspect. The inclusion of catalogue numbers, printing details etc. in the entry, therefore, does not qualify for credits. Facts which are not generally known and are brought to light as the result of careful personal enquiry by the exhibitor are certainly very creditworthy.

2 Non-Competitive Collecting

This is an important chapter for the simple reason that it concerns a lot of people. It relates to experienced collectors, would-be collectors, and those who found starting rather worrying, or began well but are now not so sure about it—perhaps housewives, or busy executives or young people in America, Great Britain or Europe. All are collectors and this is for them for it is about that most popular aspect of collecting which, largely for the matter of easy understanding, has been described in this book as non-competitive. The point was made earlier that this term has no official standing. Also, in practice, there are no hard and fast lines between competitive and non-competitive types of collecting. But, for many collectors, to be free to arrange their collections without the slightest regard for competitions is important indeed.

So far the reader has been asked to accept only the identities of the two types of collecting, and that each of them equally deserves attention. Nearly all collectors agree that they began by avoiding the seeming imponderables of the competitive world and got off the ground with a 'free-style, I-like-it-this-way' sort of collection. Of course this was rapidly improved, but even then it still could be considered as falling within the concept 'non-competitive'. It therefore seems reasonable to deal first with the non-competitive aspect of collecting.

An undeserved negative
The author considers that for such a large group of collectors to be known only by a negative attribute, i.e. non-competitive, is vastly unjust to them. It fails to signal that they have not only a very positive hobby, but also enjoy a lot more freedom than

their friends who indulge in competitions and exhibitions. Furthermore, this freedom is a highly personal one and therefore produces fun, pleasure and satisfaction. They are positive experiences and the collectors are entitled to enjoy an equally positive name for their style of collecting.

Before I began this book, a number of collectors in Great Britain were asked what name they thought best fitted the non-competitive type of collecting. All agreed that to call this free-ranging sort of collection 'non-competitive' was unsatisfactory. A number of positive suggestions were offered to them during the sampling process but none was generally acceptable. Efforts to put further pressure on another sample of collectors to accept the term 'free-range' also failed, despite the fact that this description seems to convey quite well the basic idea that the non-competitive collector is free to pick and choose his material wherever he pleases. For want of a better term therefore, the term 'non-competitive' will continue to be used in this book.

'I am an ordinary collector'

It is noticeable that occasionally there is a tendency for collectors who frequently (and sometimes very succesfully) participate in competitive collecting, to exploit and enjoy a feeling that they are superior in some way to the average 'run-of-the-mill' collector. The non-competitive collector, with his disregard for the disciplines of competitions, is apt to be looked down on and this gives him a feeling of inferiority. So when he is asked about what he collects he will reply 'I'm just an ordinary collector.' This ought to stop. He should reply that he is a non-competitive collector and that he likes it that way. If this causes the questioner to raise his eyebrows, the follow-up should be 'Well, you enjoy the competitive disciplines and I equally well like the freedom of the non-competitive for the sake of fun and pleasure.' If, for good measure, the non-competitive collector is a very good topical/thematic enthusiast, then a joint session together over their album pages might well pay very satisfactory dividends to them both.

Because the non-competitive or free-range type of collecting is being presented to the reader before the competitive, it should by no means be thought that this is the absolute order of priorities. It is fact that no such priorities have ever been established, despite the fact that some collectors would prefer to think so.

There is a considerable amount of information about the competitive world covering local competitions, national and state competitions as well as the international exhibitions in Chapters 9, 10 and 11.

It is hoped that not only the competitive enthusiasts but also the very many well-established stamp collectors will read this chapter with interest. Perhaps they may well pick up ideas which they can utilise and also secure a rather better picture of one of the other facets of the hobby.

Because it is basic, the starter-collector should try to read this chapter several times. This will undoubtedly materially increase his knowledge of the subject and widen his perspective of it. In this way his start, whether in the competitive or the non-competitive areas, will be the sounder, and the better understanding gained will help make his progress in building a satisfactory collection easier and more rewarding.

Free start, free stop

One of the biggest advantages of the non-competitive way of collecting is that work on the collection can be nicely tailored to the personal requirements of the owner. The rate of progress is entirely a matter of the collector's pleasure and opportunity. He may prefer to work at a steady pace over a number of years and then take a break until the urge to resume collecting is felt. Alternatively, there are many collectors who enjoy collecting in a series of start–stop spells, often with substantial gaps in between for other types of relaxation. Either way can produce a good collection, pleasure and satisfaction.

The author hopes that a word of caution will not be out of place here. Building a good collection requires the maintenance of certain continuities during the process. The way the items are mounted, the style of the writing-up and even the type of sheet used, all need to be the same. More important is the need to ensure that the thread of the story which the subject is to tell is not broken by the stops in collecting. Failure to look after any of these aspects can disturb the harmonious progression of the collection. So if you are thinking of having a break from collecting for a while, do try to budget for the fact that the restart will call for a certain amount of back-tracking in order to pick up the threads of continuity. It might be a good idea to make a few notes about the next few steps to be undertaken and associate these with the collection.

Equally an expert
Whether one collector enjoys the competitive area of collecting the best and another the non-competitive is certainly not the simple matter of how much expertise each has at his fingertips. In fact quite a number of enthusiasts find both types equally pleasing and attractive. There are, of course, marked differences between their collecting experiences but otherwise it is mainly that their expertise has been channeled along rather different lines.

Nor is having a very creditable knowledge of the principles of thematics and of philately the exclusive property of the competitive devotee. Many collectors who have not the slightest inclination to indulge in competitions have extensive, well-ordered collections which very clearly demonstrate that the owner has not only an excellent knowledge of the topic (or subject) but also possesses a sound grasp of the principles of thematics and philately. So there are collectors who are equally expert in the non-competitive area of collecting as in the competitive.

In the world of the non-competitive enthusiast, where the enjoyment of freedom is paramount, pleasure takes first place, with style and presentation quite a long way down the list of priorities. Thus a collection may appear at first sight to be assembled in a disastrously random way and to result from disorderly treatment. The type of sheet used can range from the bordered and highly ornamental on the one hand to the quite plain, dead white, thin card or piece of bond paper. The stamps may be completely overpowered by brilliant and highly artistic paintings or printed illustrations. In complete contrast, each stamp may be made the sole occupant of a page and thus enjoy the pride of place without the slightest interference. Some of the pages may have no writing-up on them, whilst others carry whole volumes of information, notes and remarks.

Within free-ranging, non-competitive collecting there are many ways of arranging the collection and all levels of topical/

thematic collecting to be found. Because each style, however simple or flamboyant, expresses the pleasure and enjoyment of the owner, it is, in the main, good collecting practice. Expertise is perhaps best measured by the amount of fun, enjoyment and satisfaction which the collection produces.

In a few words, the non-competitive collector may well be just as much an expert as his competitively minded colleague.

Semi-competitive

Some non-competitive collectors like the competitive style so much that they adopt it for their own use. Such collections are not only well set out, nicely arranged and in very good order but also usually quite large. They rarely remain unnoticed for long because they are so very well suited for showing at local society meetings. These audiences like to see this sort of display, mainly because it is not 'way above their heads' as so often happens when a large competitive collection is shown to them. In reality, being a semi-competitive collector with a (most creditable) foot in each camp is most enjoyable, as the author can whole-heartedly testify.

But, not all of the freestyle collections are good for showing even if they are well arranged and very presentable. To give the show satisfactorily, and make it thoroughly enjoyable to the audience, needs the right personality and ability to put it over properly. Even if the speaker has these personal attainments, his sheets and the material on them must equally well fit the bill or the event will not turn out an unqualified success after all. The semi-competitive, semi non-competitive collector certainly encounters a few restrictions on his freedom. Nevertheless, this composite collector is the happy possessor of a very satisfying niche between these two lively areas of collecting.

Are there no disadvantages?

The advantages of being a non-competitive collector have now been set out at considerable length. The pertinent question therefore is 'Are there not some disadvantages? If so what are they?' There certainly are! You may very well wish to know something about them, especially so if you are thinking of beginning to set up a collection.

First, the collecting objectives are not as evident as in the competitive area. Many thematic/topical collectors agree that they began their collecting with only the vaguest ideas as to what the end product would look like. At the start the focus is blurred by a mixture of hope and adventure; as the collection grows some of the early objectives are abandoned and new ones visualised. Not all people like things that way. They prefer to have their objectives provided for them, even if set by others. The absence of a clear focus, particularly in the early stages, spells indecision and worry for them. For these folk, much of this book is devoted to getting this worry out of the way well before the start of collecting. If, therefore, you particularly like adventures, so long as you can have a clear objective before the start, then take this book well and truly to heart. On the other hand, if you prefer to form your own objectives and can happily accept guidance, when offered, to help you come to that vital focus, then you are sitting pretty with a real collecting-type bonus, are you not?

Next, for many collectors the absence of the competitive spirit produces a loss of incentive. This is more than just not being able to obtain a high award or even an increase in collecting status. It is a clearly and well-established fact that many collectors do not only focus on the award aspect. For others competing is the strong incentive, the urge to press ahead with their entry. So it must be recognised that non-competitive collecting possesses no challenge of this kind.

Getting a good award is undoubtedly a stimulus to collecting. Nor is it practical to ignore completely the tonic effect which even an average good win can have on the entrant. As compared with stamp or postal-history collecting, arriving at the top in thematics does not usually require a lot of cash. Time, perserverance and expertise are the essentials. Pot-hunting in thematics is therefore much more creditworthy than in the other groups of collecting. The absence of this sort of 'credit peg' in non-competitive collecting is seen, by some collectors, as being something of a disadvantage.

In non-competitive collecting, the aims and ends, being not very precisely defined, bring with them the risk of the collector actually losing his way at some stage. The author remembers collections which showed very evident signs of topical/thematic wandering. Too many of these signs lead to dissatisfaction and may finally result in the end of collecting.

This absence of clear objectives may result in the collector plodding hopefully and happily along but quite unaware that, very shortly, some unseen snag will bring him to a sudden halt. When this happens the comments heard will include such as '. . . and that meant remounting and rewriting all of that part of the collection.' Sometimes this is followed by the sad remark, 'I just have not got the time to do that amount of work on the collection.' I wonder, if you were in such unfortunate and disconcerting circumstances, you would also feel that a substantial part of your collection must be actually abandoned? It is hoped that the advice in this book, especially that on selection and collection building, will save readers from experiencing such discomforts.

Another point is that the longer the collector has enjoyed the freedom of non-competitive collecting, the more difficult it will be for him to change his collecting style. If this is not in line with the competitive norm, it will call for a lot of work if he is to do well in the competition. Enforced changes in a well-established way of doing things can cause worry at the start. So the dyed-in-the-wool 'free-ranger', having a fair idea of these difficulties, keeps well out of competitive collecting. In doing so, of course, he loses the benefit of contact with a very lively, progressive and controversial facet of collecting.

Whilst there may well be some other minor disadvantages in being a non-competitive collector, those described earlier are quite representative of the types most likely to be encountered in practice. It is suggested therefore that, before the reader commits himself, he might do well to take account of each of the advantages and disadvantages already described in the light of his personal likes and dislikes. There can be no harm in asking yourself such questions as 'Do the pleasures of this type of collecting produce a real and strong response to me? Am I able to cope quite easily with the difficulties likely to arise? Shall I mind very much if the competitive collectors of my acquaintance are a bit critical of my collection?'

Whichever way you decide, thinking about these points will undoubtedly make your concept of topicals and thematics better balanced and more likely to yield a greater amount of pleasure, satisfaction and enjoyment. In other words, more fun.

To bulge or not to bulge

To be able to appreciate that the non-competitive collector has the advantage of such a great amount of freedom and also that very often he can be a real expert, certainly makes for a good understanding of thematics. But thoughts like these are theoretical and of limited practical value. The reader might well be wanting to ask the very sensible question 'If he has all of this massive freedom to enjoy, doesn't this usually result in his albums literally overflowing with a hotchpotch of stamps, covers, cancellations, slogans, postcards and so on?' Yes, it most certainly can and there is no doubt that, in this connection, the author often takes the opportunity of enjoying looking at the albums of other collectors and can recall the occasions when an owner has remarked, just before coming to a rather bulky-looking part of his collection, 'The next few sheets are where I ran wild for a bit.' Of course, he is much relieved when these pages, with a profusion of material on them, have been turned over and we are free to look at the remainder of the collection. He is, of course, very well aware that this part of the album does not do him credit and perhaps mentally notes that it must be properly cleared up before anyone else sees it. My thoughts are along that line too.

What a collection looks like, whether it first of all bulges and then overflows, will much depend on: (a) the type of item and the amount of space each requires; (b) how the items are arranged with regard to the space available on each page. At this point, how much space each item takes up is probably of the greater importance.

The line between competitive and non-competitive collecting is very indefinite at certain points and this is especially so with regard to the best kind of material to use in each case. The successful competitor will make a selection of the items to be put into his entry from approximately the same range of material as his non-competitive colleague, but with considerably more care and thought. The latter type of collector largely suits himself and if he so wishes can include everything. The following paragraphs are therefore important for all collectors and, of course, all would-be collector enthusiasts.

The following list gives the types of item from which the selection can be made:

1	Stamps as singles, pairs, blocks or panes	10	Specimens
2	First day covers	11	Semi-officials
3	Postmarks and slogans	12	Locals
4	Miniature and special sheets	13	Private postal items
5	Maximum cards	14	Fiscals
6	Postal-history items	15	Coils
7	Aerophilatelic items	16	Booklet panes
8	Postal stationery	17	Se-tenant pairs
9	Essays and proofs	18	Tête bêche pairs
		19	Gutter pairs

This list is by no means complete because there are also a number of items of a collateral nature which can be used. The term 'collateral' has been defined as anything of a non-philatelic nature included in the collection. It is much more widely used by collectors in America than in Great Britain and some further notes about this kind of material and its use will therefore be of value.

The function of collateral material is to amplify, and not merely to add an element of decoration to, the collection. Even in non-competitive collections, it should be used only when it adds to the information given by the stamps or illustrates something about one which is not self-evident. In the competitive world, some of the exhibition authorities and the judges are not prepared to accept the inclusion of collateral material whilst others will tolerate only a minimum. Clearly the collector needs to settle his own mind as to what should be included and what not in each particular case. The upper part of *Colour illustration 3* shows some very interesting collateral material.

A term not to be confused with 'collateral' and sometimes met with in Great Britain refers to 'peripheral' material. This includes postally related items which have an indirect connection with the theme or subject. Here are some of the types of collateral material in use:

1. The New Hebrides miniature sheet. The background shows the stages of the timber industry, from planting to utilisation. The designer was R. Whiteley, and the stamps were for issue in 1969

2. An attractive miniature sheet. However, it is not one that is worth including in a thematic collection

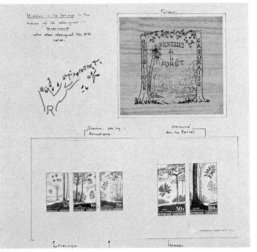

3. Use of collateral material in upper part of the sheet. Hidden in the foliage is the name of the designer, Miermont, who also designed the 5F. stamp

4. Example of the term 'freak'

5. A good maximum card. This example, of the Valais viaduct at Lötschberg, has a positive value because the train element is clearer and the cancellation is a good depictic of the viaduct

1	Postcards	8	Bank notes and
2	Photographs		Treasury bills
3	Documents	9	Shares and other
4	Drawings and diagrams		certificates
5	Paintings	10	Coins
6	News cuttings		
7	Press and other official announcements		

It must be agreed that these two lists add up to a sizeable amount from which the collector can make a selection when building his collection. Providing he notes that quite a number of these should be used sparingly and with care, every reasonable advantage should be taken of this very wide range of material to ensure that the pages show plenty of variety and interest. In this way, the maximum amount of enjoyment and fun will be obtained not only during building the collection but when looking at it thereafter. But the point must be made with some emphasis that variety is not the only thing to keep in mind. The most important is the end product: a well set-up and attractive collection which is also satisfactory from the topical/thematic point of view.

The fact that in order to achieve thematic acceptability some sorts of items may be used only with care means knowing those which can be safely used in the collection and those which, because they have a secondary importance, must be looked at critically before they are included or even left out completely. Needless to say, it is much better if discrimination is exercised before purchase and not after it. It does not make for the happiest sort of collecting to realise these differences, as to what should be in and what properly out, some time after the collection has been assembled and the earlier pages, with their misfits, are well established in the collection. Nor is it good for the pocket!

Put simply, the decision whether to buy or not hangs on three very simple axioms. These are:

1 That, although the stamp's the thing, getting the right ones in the right places is the priority.
2 That you decide before the purchase how relevant an

item is to the theme/topical/subject and where it will fit into the collection.

3   That there are advantages to be gained from taking into account the effects of both the size and the colour of each item on the layout of each page and on the collection as a whole.

Undoubtedly, the stamp is the king of the collection. But even the most minor of monarchs must be seen to possess the requisite qualities and so be worthy of an honourable place. Nor is it fitting for a king to be overshadowed by his associates. Here are some of the thoughts about the place of the stamp in the collection.

The stamp's the thing

In topical/thematic circles, the popular catch phrase is 'the stamp's the thing' and without doubt it is an almost complete requirement that the significance of the stamp components on an album sheet should dominate that of all the others. The possible exception? Clearly, when the subject or theme has a strong postal-history content and covers are very largely employed, some amount of departure is quite permissible. The use of slogans to develop a theme or show a subject also comes in this category.

That the stamps should predominate holds in both general and particular cases and this applies whether they are unused (as most should be) or on covers, pieces, as essays, proofs or specimens. Therefore, whenever doubt arises as to what should or should not be included on a page, settle it in the first instance by applying the maxim that 'the stamp's the thing'. This is the primary test. Others will be described later on in this chapter.

If any item on a page tends to reduce or destroy the importance of the stamp components then something is wrong and must be put right. For example, a stamp of small format, but which is making a material contribution to the theme, subject or topic, could well be completely overshadowed by a nearby large, bright maximum card. If this card is making only a rather minor contribution to the progress of the subject the case for its retention on this page is not at all good. To let the stamp enjoy its proper significance it might be wise to remove the card to a separate page where its significance can be strengthened. Of course, that small but important stamp will now need some support, preferably by other stamps. All of this clearly calls for the redesign of several pages of the collection. Even so, the prospect of having to do this extra work should not be seen as a deterrent because one of the fundamental points in thematics, that the stamp's the thing, is at stake.

What about the reverse side of the coin where the maximum card or FDC etc. is going to be of far greater importance than the stamps? Or when it is desired to put a document of considerable size, capable of making a massive contribution to the progress of the collection, on the same sheet as one or two stamps of some importance? What is the collector to do about such items? Buy them or leave them? Now, as is quite usual with questions of this kind, each must be considered on its merits. First, if it is quite impossible to replace the document or large item by stamps without loss of thematic worth, you have no alternative but to grant it a proper place in your collection. If it is both large and bright, thereby compelling attention, the best solution is to mount it solo on a separate sheet. If very conveniently it is less commanding of attention, it can be given pride of place on a sheet with no more than one or two stamps in support if need be. An excellent example which adds to the thematic merit is shown in *Colour illustration 5*.

It is hoped that the reader will notice that in the first example, where the small but important stamp was seen to be overshadowed by the large maximum card, the collector was involved in quite a lot of inconvenience to put things right. In the second case, however, the question of predominance was noticed before the mounting-up had been done. This latter course has the advantage of saving time, trouble and inconvenience. In terms of pleasure, fun and satisfaction the exercise of foresight in this way is surely worthwhile. So the discriminating collector, and that's certainly you by now, will appreciate that there is a bit more to 'the stamp's the thing' than appears at first sight.

Now for another thought which bears rather indirectly on that much discussed subject of overcrowding. The easy axiom that 'the stamp's the thing' ought not to be used as a blanket authority that all stamps, irrespective of the degree to which they are relative to the theme, subject or topical are right for inclusion in the collection. In the Introduction, the example of ships on stamps was used to establish, first that those items which clearly advance the theme or add materially to the subject or topical collection by showing a new facet or another angle cannot be left out. Not that, within limits, this applies equally well to groups of stamps with the same or somewhat similar design when, by so doing, the breaking of a set is avoided. The Introduction also made the important point that not all stamps contribute an equal amount to the advancement of the subject. In fact, when the thematic detail is smaller, indistinct, the stamp is of little or no use in the collection.

The reader may well be tempted to ask the question, 'Then where does the line of inclusion or exclusion, in practice, really fall?' The answer to this is that much depends on the degree of relevance which each item possesses, whether it be a stamp, cover or any other item of that long list given earlier in the chapter. Perhaps this matter of degrees of relevance will be worthwhile looking at objectively. Why not?

Degrees of relevance
When assessing the topical/thematic merit of a stamp or item, with a view to the inclusion in the collection, the author has adopted three categories of relevance for his personal use. Moreover, he makes a strong point of not overlooking them when buying is in mind. Here they are:

Category 1
This contains all those items which exhibit such a strong connection with the theme/topic/subject that they cannot but make a major contribution to the progress of the collection. If they are not included, the collection is the poorer! So thinking runs along the following lines. If the item will fit very nicely into the topical, or show the subject clearly and without doubt, or helps along the story of the theme in a logical way, then it is right for inclusion. Doubtless the reader will rapidly bring to mind plenty of examples which nicely fit this bill. Here are two from the 'Trees and Humanity' collection of the 'Symbolic Tree' section. They are shown in *Illustrations 2.1* and *2.2*. The first symbolises the tree as 'steadfast and strong' whilst the

second shows a cachet depicting Ireland at the top of the 'tree' of the European Economic Community.

Category 2
This includes all those items, stamps, covers and the like which show some secondary connection with subject. Often the elements which are so useful to the collector appear for no other than artistic purposes and are ancillary to the main design. The first example (*Illustration 2.3*) shows a cachet on an FDC which, in view of the title of the picture 'The Madonna of the Trees' and also because of the inclusion of the stylised trees in the background, was found a suitable niche (and no more) in the section of the collection for 'Trees in Art'. The trees in the painting are of minor artistic value and the title was applied mainly for purposes of distinction. A much better place for this cover would be, of course, in a collection of religion or art on stamps.

The second (*Illustration 2.4*) is the front of the folder enclosing the Jersey nineteenth-century farming issue of stamps. It is a bright and attractive item but is non-postal and therefore properly suitable for a non-competitive collection. The trees are large and distinctive but are somewhat accidental to both the stamps and the motif of the folder. When the owner was asked why this item was included in the collection, the reply came: 'First of all it shows the tree in winter and in a countryside setting. So far I have not been able to find a stamp which shows this so well and so attractively.' Then an afterthought was added which surprised me: 'You see, I put what I like in my collection.' Knowing that the collection was never designed for competitive use, the author wholeheartedly supported this comment.

Items in Category 2 call for much more discrimination than those in 1. This is mainly because of the very large number of marginal cases which come to the notice of the collector. He frequently has to ask himself whether an item really belongs to his collection; how strong is the case for inclusion. Then where can it be put? To help answer these questions, use might be made of the following guidelines. The connection with the subject, topical or theme must be (a) positive and capable of recognition in detail in order that it can be adequately described in the writing-up; (b) sufficiently strong to allow the position in the collection and the function of the item in the logical progress to be clearly established.

Experience shows that the use of guidelines such as these does not impose the slightest restriction on the collector's freedom. The author finds them invaluable. This is because he made them and you are just as free to do the same for yourself, of course.

Category 3
This includes the kind of item which, although it has some connection with the subject, the relationship is so poor that nothing would be gained by its inclusion in the collection. The detail relative to the subject may well be so indistinct that proper recognition is impossible. Such an item can neither have a place in the collection nor can it be written up satisfactorily. Despite this, stamps of this sort are often put into a collection for no better reason than that they are reputed to have a collecting potential and their market value will appreciate in the future. A far better place for this item is in the stockbook.

What about the stamp or cover which is bright and attractive but whose connection with the topical/subject again is only some very minor and insignificant detail? Providing that competitive use is not contemplated and it is quite positive that you would derive pleasure and satisfaction from putting it into the collection, even if there is no philatelic reason, go ahead and give the item a place where it pleases you the most. But do try to remember precisely why you have made use of it—very possibly you may well have a different idea about it one day!

Although there is no clear line between items in Categories 1, 2 and 3, this does not invalidate their use whenever possible. Their value to the collector lies in the fact that items in Category 1 are capable of adding considerably more to the progress of the collection than those in Category 3. It is therefore very easy to distinguish between a stamp clearly in Category 1 and another which undoubtedly falls into Category 3. Those in the first group are the best buys, and if those in Category 3 are not taken no harm is done to the collection by the non-inclusion. In fact the margin between these two is so great that it requires only a little thought when a purchase is in mind to settle the matter either way. As regards items which are not in either Category 1 or Category 3, you are free to pick and choose much as your fancy dictates. Occasionally, however, an inspired purchase will produce a much more valuable contribution to the progress of the theme or topical than was first thought on casual inspection. Research into the background of a stamp, the reason for the inclusion of apparently minor details by the designer and other clues are often invaluable in the process of evaluating the relevance to the subject.

In conclusion, the benefits of using a scale of relevancies of this sort are:

1   The thematic quality of the collection is improved, i.e. the steps of the story which the stamps etc. are required to tell are clear and easy to follow and this results in a high yield of fun, pleasure and enjoyment.

2   It helps to reduce the possibility of overcrowding. The thought behind this is that it is currently considered to be good practice to allow very important items to have plenty of space on the pages of the collection and the lesser lights a rather smaller amount of elbow room. A reduction in the number of items of this latter type therefore helps to reduce overcrowding.

3   Last, but by no means least, the collector develops the ability to spot the items which are going to help his collection substantially and to buy them 'on the spot' rather than take the risk of losing them, Additionally, fewer items of relatively low value to the progress of the subject are bought. In day-to-day phraseology, he gets a better collection for less money.

The importance of size and colour
When you are designing a page of the album—that is deciding which stamps, covers and other items are to be chosen and where they are to be placed—one of the important factors concerns two of the very common physical features of each item, or rather the combination of them: (a) the effect of the size; and (b) the impact of the colour. If your comment at this point is along the lines of 'Yes, they may very well be important, but do I really have to go into this at all? Can't I forget it completely and get straight on with the job of putting the

stamps and covers just where I think they should go on the pages?' As a happy, free-ranging, non-competitive collector the only thing essential is to enjoy yourself. All the same, a little later on you may well discover that thought about size and colour, before doing the mounting-up, can be very much to your advantage. On the other hand, if you have even the remotest idea of entering a competition (and that's the same as exhibiting) you should try to take the matter much more seriously. For you to disregard the effects of size and colour at the design stage could well mean many regrets later on. So please read on with care.

The next point is that taking account of the importance of the size of an item and its colour is largely a matter of common sense. Maybe you have just not thought about them before? The dimensions of some of the items in the collection may well be many times greater than those of others. Thus the usual FDC is about 20 times the size of a stamp of the average format. So some six or seven stamps, reasonably spaced, could be shown in the same space as the cover would occupy. In other words, the cover or other similarly large item prevents the use of at least six stamps, each of which might well illustrate a different angle of the subject or show another example to reinforce an idea. The vital question therefore is 'Does this cover, this large miniature sheet or other item, really justify its inclusion in the collection?'

Consideration of size is very much the matter of how much space on a sheet each item consumes. At the bottom end of the range, and requiring the very minimum of space, are the midget-like bantams of South Africa or the early issues of some of the South American countries. There are many contenders for the top place. Claims to have issued the world's largest stamp occur quite regularly but in the long run it is the commercial cover which consumes the greatest amount of space on an album page.

To the eye, the very large item seems to take up a disproportionate amount of space and to reduce the remaining area available for smaller ones equally quickly. This results in an unfortunate distortion of the general impression of the sheet which argues further against the use of over-large items.

Although size is of first importance, it cannot properly be taken into account without considering the effect of colour.

Strongly coloured stamps are much more attractive to the eye than those which are pale and insipid. A vivid or very bright stamp amongst a group of less highly coloured items seems to demand attention and this may well be wrong for the logical understanding of the story the page is designed to tell. It is even more against this attention-demanding stamp that it tends to hold the eye overlong, possibly to the detriment of other items. *Illustration 2.5* shows such a group with a bright and attractive stamp at the centre. It is generally accepted that, other things being equal, an item at the middle of a page will command the most attention. So, if all the stamps on the sheet have equal thematic merit, those above the centre and those below it are at an optical disadvantage. The average viewer will nearly always commence to look at this array of stamps at the centre and not, as is correct, at the top left-hand side. How soon he corrects this is mostly a personal matter. Inevitably there is disturbance of the concentration, resulting in loss of appreciation and pleasure. (Note that an example of a solution of a colour objectivity problem is given in *Colour illustration 12.*)

However, not all people have the same degree of response to bright, attractive colours. Sometimes the strong, bright colour may have little or no attraction or even act as a repellant. *Illustration 2.6*, with the brilliant stamp at the centre, does not always produce the same strong reaction in each person as was described earlier. Please try to remember this point when letting another collector look through your collection and also try to make allowances for this different optical capability when you are browsing over that of another because it can make a vast amount of difference as to how often you see eye-to-eye with each other.

Combining the effects of size and colour

Up to this point it has been noted that size consumes space and colour compels interest. In practice, of course, these two properties are inseparable and it is therefore essential that the reader should know something about the combined effects of size and colour. At the top end of the scale there are the very large and very bright items such as a big block of highly coloured stamps or an outsized and highly ornamental cover.

Here we have maximum size combined with maximum attraction. Together, they double the dose af attractiveness. At the bottom end and with the very minimum capability to attract attention is the small, very pale, stamp. Here the double dose is not of attractiveness but of insignificance. In between these two limits there are innumerable gradations, each produced by the combination of size and colour.

To get down to practicalities, let us suppose that a working answer is needed in the case where a sheet is to show, in the following order, two pale and not very large stamps followed by a special strip of stamps all of which are bright, attractive and will occupy a sizeable amount of space. *Illustration 2.6* shows the effect of mounting these three items straight on to a sheet without regard to the effects of size and colour. The long bright strip of stamps tends to call for first attention and thus disturbs the proper sequence of the items on the sheet. It will also continue to hold the attention to the disadvantage of the two quite important stamps at the top of the page. The question is, 'What steps can be taken to reduce the total visual impact of the strip of stamps and at the same time to increase that of the two singles above it?' The object is to rearrange the items so that the two stamps secure the prior attention and so ensure that the story which this sheet is to tell is logically correct and clear.

This problem page could be tackled as follows. First, lower the long strip of stamps on the page so that it is well out of the way of the focal point at the centre. Next, mount the two small stamps on a black background, allowing them a fairly generous border. Doing this will increase their apparent size and hence make them more likely to attract attention. The last step is to integrate them, by means of a block or writing-up, so that the whole forms an area which has roughly the same attraction as that of the block of stamps situated in the lower half of the sheet. The rearranged layout helps the eye to start looking at the top of the page rather than at the big strip of stamps at the middle.

A cogent point is, does the enthusiastic collector really have to stop to take account of this size and colour effect before making each and every purchase? What are the priorities? Of course, it would undoubtedly be most convenient if just those items which do not produce this size/colour problem could be secured at one purchase. But the collector experiences difficulties enough in finding sufficient suitable material without being so highly selective about it.

The first priority for the non-competitive collector is undoubtedly to buy the material as and when it comes up for sale but with the two easy provisos: (a) that it is relative to his theme/topical/subject; and (b) that it is a good buy in terms of pleasure, enjoyment and satisfaction. After that it is a matter of taste and skill as to whether the effects of size and colour are noticed. It is a part of collecting freedom to be sensitive or insensitive to them. So by all means arrange your collection entirely to your own liking and take account of size and colour if and when the need arises. But do try to remember that others may see its bright colours and large items somewhat differently from you. To those who are competition conscious, completely to ignore the combined effects of size and colour may well result in a disappointment and very possibly a disaster. To suffer these is not good collecting. The author accordingly suggests that rather than run the risk of such unwelcome experiences, food for thought may well be found in Chapter 3.

The risk of indigestion

It is impossible not to notice that there are many collectors who, right from the start, like to cram each album page with stamps, covers, cancellations, photographs, drawings and other sorts of items. Then the writing-up is squeezed into every unoccupied space so that the sheet is completely and absolutely full. Nothing gives them so much pleasure as the sight of these sheets, each quite full from edge to edge and top to bottom with the widest possible range of material. The brighter it is the better. These collectors need space to put stamps into, not space without them, and the picturesque bordered sheets are therefore quite inadequate for their needs. Here the author is quite positive on one point: if this style of collecting will make and keep them happy and satisfied, then it is certainly fine for them. It's their collection.

Experience shows, however, that very often, many of these collectors find themselves, a little later on, wishing to make a change in the style of mounting and of writing-up. The pages appear to have lost a lot of their attractiveness. Why? Of course there are very good reasons for this but the plain fact is that because the items are so close together it is difficult to make out what contribution each is producing to the story of the collection. At first it was the attraction of the masses of stamps and the bright colours which made such a strong appeal. Now, experience has softened this impact and allowed the importance of the stamp and its story to come through. So it is the details of the stamps, as well as their general impression, which is so vital. Inevitably they come to the conclusion that it would have been far better to have allowed much more space between the items right from the start. Then they could be seen properly. But the prospect of having to reorganise the whole of the collection from the beginning is not a pleasant one and therefore so easy to put off until 'another day'.

The arrival of new material for the collection compels the collector to make a decision of sorts. In the future all the items must be spaced much more generously and the writing-up must be kept within reasonable limits. One can easily envisage the owner saying to himself that this is the right way to set up a good collection and now he is happy again. But what about those sheets at the front of the collection which are so very badly overcrowded? Sometimes the collector will try to avoid looking at them or even pretend that they do not exist. He is even less happy about them when he comes to realise that they cannot be removed from the album because they are the beginning of the story, the launching pad of his collection. The very sight of the pages in question gives him no pleasure whatever and they are easily liable to give him that unpleasant complaint of philatelic indigestion.

It goes without saying that it would have been far better to have avoided this most uncomfortable complaint than to have to endure the cure for it. To be in this unfortunate position is, at best, an unsatisfactory and unprofitable way of gaining experience. By being a little more wise at the start, by taking better note of what more experienced collectors do, as well as the advice in so many of the handbooks, all the annoying and troublesome effects of overcrowding can be avoided. The reader can get an idea of the state of the album pages before and after the cure for this particular sort of indigestion from *Illustration 2.7* and *2.8*.

Going competitive

Starting a non-competitive collection always brings a lot of fun and pleasure. The new interest produces an exciting kind of activity and the freedoms it opens up for the collector are very pleasant. All of these are good for the enthusiasm too. At this point, the influence of this new way of collecting is so strong that very often a change of any sort is the last thing envisaged.

Collecting is a progressive activity and the outlook changes and improves as more and more of the topical/thematic world is recognised and evaluated. The important fact is that practical skill and collecting expertise also continue to increase. Then, by almost imperceptible steps, the collector sees the need for improvements in the style of his sheets. Alterations and experiments are made, various types of layout and writing-up are tried. So, bit by bit his focus is changed until a happy solution is reached. Then, ostensibly to look over the stock of the dealers, a visit is made to one of the big exhibitions. During this, an unexpected discovery is made when he sees, very clearly, that there is a good measure of similarity between his album sheets and those on show in the exhibition. This sets him thinking: 'Why should I not have a shot at entering next year? This may well mean a bit of effort on my part but then I may well win a medal.'

On the way home there are more thoughts about it and the practical ones are high on the list of priorities. The first of course is the important one of what work has to be done on the sheets of his collection between now and the closing date. So, for the first time, he will have to work to a target, to hunt out the rules and regulations, to find material and to make plans.

Soon he arrives at the stage when an attempt is made to align his sheets with the judging criteria. Now comes the need to know the precise meaning of such terms as presentation, condition, philatelic knowledge and and general impression. Next, where can he discover all this sort of information? Hard on the heels of all of this are the thoughts about time to do all the work and the cost in cash and pleasure.

Let us be practical. The answers to many of these questions can be found in two places. The first is in this book, with the aid of the Bibliography. The other is the rough-and-tumble world of experience. Both are complementary and are invaluable. So, if you are contemplating an entry into the competitive world of collecting, you may well like to spend a bit of your time over the several chapters ahead. Doing so may help you to avoid having such thoughts as 'Unfortunately I did not appreciate that it would work out so disappointingly.' How pleasant it would be if you were able to replace this by 'Yes I had an idea that it could well go this way and happily it has.'

A last thought before the next chapter. Does this new way of collecting of necessity mean the loss of most of the fun and pleasure which comes from collecting? The exact answer depends a good deal on your perspective, your resilience and your enthusiasm. Competitive collecting can be as enjoyable as the non-competitive. It is certainly progressive, stimulating and rewarding. These are excellent ingredients for pleasure and satisfaction.

---

3 Competitive Collecting

The world of competitive collecting

Competitive collecting is a world-wide activity. It has a coverage which is geographical not only in area but also as regards the level and the type of competition. Thus, wherever an international exhibition is to be staged, the 56 nations currently members of the international philatelic federation (FIP) pledge their support. The extent and importance of these internationals can be judged from the fact that they are carefully arranged well in advance so that each country gets the opportunity to stage an exhibition in turn. At the other end of the scale there are small groups of enthusiasts in almost every country in the world who enjoy organising and entering local competitive events annually or even more frequently. In total, these very ordinary competitions must involve many millions of collectors. Between these two extremes—the massive international exhibition and the small local competition—there is, of course, a whole range of competitive events from those of the many federations or associations of the counties, regions and states to the relatively large national exhibitions. Competitive collecting can therefore be justly said to command world-wide popularity.

In the same way that non-competitive collectors enjoy fun, pleasure and freedoms, so competitive enthusiasts secure their share of excitement, satisfaction and rewards from the preparation and submission of their exhibits. This broad picture of collectors throughout the world, each drawing his dividend of pleasure, is one which is so often completely overlooked. This is perhaps the greatest commendation possible for competitive collecting.

This book, with no less than four chapters devoted to the

subject, offers the reader the widest possible coverage of competitive thematics. The order in which these four chapters are placed corresponds to the practical pattern of collecting, in that the sheets submitted for the competition are usually in the nature of an extension of an ordinary collection. This chapter, which introduces the subject, is therefore placed before Chapters 4 to 8, which deal with finance, selection, collecting methods and collection building respectively. The remaining three chapters about different levels of competitive collecting then follow. *Illustration 3.1* shows the arrangement.

It should be particularly noted that the titles of these three chapters were chosen as a matter of convenience and that the coverage of each is wider than indicated. In both Great Britain and America the current organisational linkages, and the catchment areas from which entries for competitions are received, are quite diverse in character. Thus, societies may be local or super-national. Associations cover a very wide variety of organisations. For example, the American Topical Association has a world-wide coverage and the American Philatelic Society has more than 600 chapters in its organisation. Both bodies run competitive events. In Great Britain there is no equivalent of the American Topical Association, which caters exclusively for topical collectors. The Royal Philatelic Society of London does not run any competitive events directly, but provides massive support for the national exhibitions.

Opportunity will be given at the commencement of each of these chapters for the reader to visualise the type and level of the event which it covers and how the best possible use can be made of the information included.

At this point the author proposes to take the liberty of suggesting that all the readers of this book, irrespective of whether they have competing in mind or not, should become acquainted with the background of the competitive side of collecting. In this way, they may well be adding something to their thematic stature. Much can be discovered from the very simple question 'Why is it so exciting, rewarding and satisfying?' Broadly speaking, there are three types of human experience, all of which can contribute to produce the sum total of these very human pleasures. They are: (a) the benefits which

7. A specialised pictorial sheet

6. A group of fully pictorial and bordered sheets

8. Discreet background on a sheet in a Copernicus collection

9. A miniature sheet with maximum thematic merit. Trees of each country; British Honduras. This miniature sheet, designed and signed by Jennifer M. Toombs, shows the trees, their fruits or flowers, and the types of wood they yield

10. Introduction sheet for non-competitive collection

— The Tree and Mankind —
The collection is arranged on the following basis:
1.   Introduction
2.   British Tree
3.   Trees as a Source of Food
4.   The Timber Industry
5.   Timber Supplies, Use, etc
6.   The Trees of Each Country
7.   Symbolic Trees
8.   Conservation
9.   Trees in Scenes, etc
10.   Slogans & Postmarks
11.   Miscellaneous Aspects
12.   Flowering Trees

PARAGUAY · G. 0.20

The leaves in the tail

The Tree and Mankind
The Collection from which this entry has been drawn comprised of eleven divisions, as follows:
1. British trees.   2. Trees as a source of f
3. The timber industry.   4. Timber supplies and use
5. The trees of each country. 6. Symbolic Trees.
7. Conservation.   8. Trees in scenes on stan
9. Slogans & Postmarks.   10. Miscellaneous aspects
            11. Flowering Trees
This entry is made up of part of Division No.1, Briti
It shows (a) Trees on stamps; (b) Trees on other post
(c) Trees on the 1966 landscape stamps; (d) Conserv
(e) Symbolic stamps.

(a). Trees on British Stamps
                Oak

            laurel

11. Introduction sheet as modified for a competition entry

1772-75 James Cook Just over 200 years ago Captain James Cook, in the H.M.S.Resolution, began his last and greatest voyage to the Pacific. During the southern summers of 1772-73 and 1773-74 he circumnavigated the southern oceans and crossed the Antarctic Circle for the first time in history on Jan 17th 1773, dispelling the idea of a southern continent extending to the temperate latitudes.

            Def Issue   Feb 66

Bicentenary of Capt Cook's Circumnavigation of the Antarctic Sep 72

Bicentenary of Capt Cook's Crossing of Antarctic Circle   Jan 73

Landed in South Georgia and took possession for King George III in Possession Bay on 17th Jan 1775:

Bicentenary of Capt Cook's Discovery of South Georgia   Apr 75

12. A well-balanced sheet

result or are conferred; (b) the advantages which can be taken or accrued; and (c) the motives which will be satisfied. The first can be personal or impersonal, The personal benefits are widely experienced but it is the latter type, the impersonal, which are so often overlooked. Organised collecting is usually very productive of good and long-lasting progress and it therefore makes a substantial contribution to the progress of the hobby as a whole. The organisers of exhibitions arrange the show with two ideas in mind. The first, of course, is to cater for the competitive requirements. The other is quite different. This is primarily to interest the public and at the same time to give them an opportunity to see for themselves the relationship between the entries and the awards. With these in mind, a complete range of award-winning entries is put on show up to the maximum capacity of the venue. This contrast facility is one of the invaluable contributions which an exhibition can make to collecting and collectors. Further, it is important to note that the efforts of the competitors to secure better awards has the result of progressively raising the standard of the material entered for the show. The exhibition of their work makes this progressive pattern, this evidence of increasing merit, available to the other exhibitors and the public as a whole. This wide, impersonal type of benefit is rarely ever counted in real terms in the press, philatelic or everyday. Indeed, it would be rather difficult to do so, but it must be acknowledged that the measure of the direct and indirect advantages to the hobby which result must be very large indeed. Most competitors find it essential to concentrate entirely on the work of completing their entry and it is quite natural therefore that the broader benefits which derive to the public and the other competitors should rarely come to mind. This certainly conveys no discredit whatsoever to the collectors involved. Quite the contrary, they deserve every commendation.

The personal benefits and advantages are not only numerous but also somewhat diverse in character. This is not unusual because humanity likes, enjoys and thrives on variety. Here are some thoughts about the personal benefits and advantages of competitive collecting.

Probably the most important benefit derived from competing is the stimulating effect which can be produced by winning an award. Frequently, to secure one right at the very bottom of the scale will result in just as great a tonic to the collector as taking one at the very top. Enthusiasm receives a boost and there is a substantial increase in interest and pleasure. The owner enjoys the thought that he has learned a lot more about collecting, while the feeling that both his status and that of his collection have been materially improved is very satisfying.

Entering a competition can produce a peak of pleasure. If the collector normally leads a very quiet, 'come day, go day' sort of existence, these outbursts of fun and excitement could be regarded as mild thematic kicks. In this way, some collectors go from one event to another, one peak of pleasure to the next, over a period of several years until they become a victim of competitive exhaustion. Their look-back picture, full of highlights if not successes, remains bright and sustaining for a very long time.

Often there is a strong element of satisfaction just in entering a competition and the enthusiast soon finds that enjoying a series of peak satisfactions can be very pleasant indeed. Happy collectors! When they sense that they are nearing the ceiling of their capacity and that the climax is not too far away, then the most pleasant of endings 'produces itself'. So they adopt a formula such as 'Just this once more and then I shall be entirely satisfied.' Experience shows that they nearly always are!

Here is a very different aspect of competitive thematics. Very few collectors have either the time or money to raise the whole of their collection to the very high level required for a good competitive entry. But a vast number of them are easily able to concentrate over just sufficient sheets to allow an entry to be constructed. In this way, a bright and attractive section of the collection is produced which, without the competition, would have been denied to them. Even if it is on a somewhat restricted scale, this is certainly a good method of enjoying pleasure and, the more times it occurs, the better for the collector.

Many collectors do not enjoy an open-ended type of activity such as is produced by the non-competitive type of collecting. They much prefer to embark upon a commitment of definite duration so that they can feel free thereafter. Thus, the competition or exhibition, with its fixed date for the latest submission of an entry, fits their bill excellently and they will beaver away unremittingly at the task against the day of freedom. This cycle of 'work–relax, work–relax' is typical of much human life. To the author it conjures up the picture of the collector warming his toes by the fire of his thematic efforts after a long spell of hard work. This is something he has every right to enjoy.

In somewhat the same human area, there are many collectors who vastly enjoy the competitive spirit as such. They like the challenge it produces and the sight of a target to aim at. In particular, it satisfies those quite unusual people who happily admit that 'they work better when they are compelled to' or that 'they like to have something against which they must work.' This sort of enthusiasm is evident at all levels of competition and is certainly not restricted to the big international events. In the practical world of collecting it is not so much the reason but the end product which counts and some of these 'compelled' entries are to be found amongst the top flights in many exhibitions.

Now for some of the more mundane but practical aspects of exhibiting. Probably at the top of this list is the fact that many collectors take part in competitive events for no other reason than to secure a creditable award, a medal and possibly a trophy. The right to look forward to a good win, to contemplate the receipt of the good news and later on the award itself is only one of the pleasures conferred on the competition entrants.

A high-level win undoubtedly adds to the status of both collector and collection, but some qualification may be called for when assessing the degree of benefit conferred. Successive wins will undoubtedly draw the collector into a more élite but smaller circle of acquaintances. Unless the collector has a very kindly spirit and a likeable personality it may seem that the rest of the world appears to have taken a visible step away from him; some in respect, but others in envy. The author's recommendation about this state of affairs is first to go in for all the competitions and exhibitions you wish, regardless of the calls of 'pot-hunter' by others. That's your right. But try to restrict that inevitable publicity so that the more wins you achieve the less is known about them by the rest of the world. Then you can make the most of them as large and important slices of your personal pleasure.

Exhibitions and competitions also provide the very valuable facility that by this means one competitor can compare his work with that of others. To take full advantage of this means, of course, devoting sufficient time both for the travelling involved and for making the all-important comparison exercise. To be really effective, the latter must be carried out very thoroughly and it is wise not to underestimate the amount of time required. To plan to spend at least one day at a national or other large exhibition and three days at an international is by no means over generous. Preferably with the help of a knowledgeable companion the rest of the entries in the same class can be examined critically and the prospects assessed for a better award 'next time'. American competitors have an additional facility open to them in that they can attend the special judging critiques and so gain further advice and information about the techniques of competing. These facilities for position-fixing and prospect-assessing are valuable advantages which accrue to collectors who participate in competitive activities. It is on record that many of the top exhibitors agree that they owe much of their success to these facilities.

The successive levels of competitive collecting, from the local society event at the bottom to the international exhibition at the top, should not be envisaged as a kind of ladder with a continuous series of rungs or steps. Obtaining a good award at one level does not always confer the right to enter the next higher event. There are, however, two points at which this kind of privilege can be enjoyed. These are: (a) in the United States an award of 'champion in show' at one of the major recognised events carries with it the right to participate in the annual 'champion of champions' competition; (b) in the regulations which govern international exhibitions it is stated that the normal requirement before an application for an entry can be submitted to the exhibition authorities is that the award of a silver medal (at least) at a national exhibition (or the equivalent) shall have been made. Despite the fact that these regulations are restrictive, the primary object is that they should produce both general and personal benefits. That they do so is self-evident.

So much for the credit or benefit aspect of competing. The wise collector will also take into account the other side of the coin, the risks, disadvantages and disappointments of competitive collecting. Here are some points for thought.

First, good thematic entries are expensive to plan, produce and enter. This is particularly so in respect of the nationals, the large 'state' and the international exhibitions. In the latter, where upwards of 100 sheets of top quality may be exhibited, the whole process of planning, preparing and entering could well require a period of time well in excess of a year. Moreover, because of the need to observe a latest date for submission of the entry, the collector is not entirely free to do the work at any pace he pleases. Even the best of estimates as to when to commence the job of preparing the entry can be disastrously upset by a multitude of unforeseen difficulties and obstacles. The wise exhibitor can usually foresee some of the difficulties and disappointments. The balance he must endure.

Compared with stamp or postal-history entries, those in the thematic class are by no means as expensive to get together. Over and above the cost of special material, the expenses which must be incurred for frame fees, insurance and postage or conveyance can amount to quite a sizeable sum. This is fine if a good win and award result, but what if it goes the other way? Then the average collector tends to regard these expenses as rather unsatisfactory losses and the whole exercise to be decidedly unpalatable. He probably considers that it would have been far better to have spent the money involved on material for the collection and this adds fuel to the fires of his disappointment. The author can recall a number of instances where a collector suffers such a severe disappointment at not getting the award on which he had set his heart, and which has cost him so much time and money, that he becomes quite disheartened. In due course he recovers his former enthusiasm, but in the interval his collecting activity remains very much in the doldrums. So, if you aim for the higher levels of pleasure, excitement and enthusiasm, you must expect to have to pay for them in one way or another.

The rules and regulations for competitions are usually set out very clearly for the guidance of intending competitors. To these must be added an understanding of the judging criteria set for the event, most of which employ a special terminology. For instance, what precisely is meant by 'presentation' or 'general impression'? What constitutes 'philatelic knowledge' in the

thematic world? There is even more to this picture. Each level
of competition, even in the same country, may call for entirely
different thinking. All these, the rules and regulations, the
judging criteria and the 'understandings', add up to a code of
discipline which the intending competitor, if he is to be
successful, must find the time and interest to master.
Furthermore, he must repeat this process when he
contemplates moving to a higher level. Mastering these
disciplines is not a question of unravelling secrets. It is much
the matter of having the time, the patience and sufficient
enthusiasm to visit every exhibition far and near, to take advice
and use it to advantage, to persevere and to refuse to 'call it a
day' until the coveted award has been won. If competitive
collecting is to remain a happy experience, then these very
personal expenditures may not be overlooked.

The reader should now have a fairly good picture of the
background of competitive collecting and doubtless will now
wish to have information of a more specific and practical
nature. This is contained in Chapters 9, 10 and 11.

SOME LIGHT RELIEF
At this point in the book, the reader is thoroughly entitled to
some form of light relief. Chapters 1, 2 and 3 contain a lot
of vital information covering both philately and thematics/
topicals. Collecting is for pleasure, however, and the author
therefore takes the liberty of suggesting that sight of *Illustration
3.2* will act as a reminder that the lighter side of our hobby is
as important as the more serious.

---

4   Cash and Collecting

Most collectors consider that their first objective is to make the maximum possible progress with their collection whilst others regard the satisfactory preparation of entries to competitions and exhibitions as the major job. In both cases it is the measure of pleasure and enjoyment produced that matters.

Nowadays, however, the general trend of human affairs appears to place more and more importance on money. The 'experts' consider that we are now well advanced into a phase of money-plus-value consciousness. The author, being a collector at heart, has no public views on this very interesting statement. On the other hand, he is quite sure that the correct position for a chapter on finance in this book, with its ongoing concept, is immediately before that on collection building. This arrangement is merely a matter of finding the most appropriate place for it and certainly not to try to persuade readers that they should count their money before they spend it! Many books on stamp collecting contain no more than a few random thoughts about finance and some nothing at all on any of the many cost aspects of collecting. Do these authors ever read the auction sale catalogues and the prices realised, or do they pretend that money is not required and does not even exist?

It is accordingly hoped that readers will find this chapter to be of interest and substantial value in their collecting.

Very few collectors allow themselves to be seriously concerned with the financial side of the hobby; in fact many have not the slightest interest in it at all! There are, however, two thoughts which occur occasionally to most. The first relates to the average cost of getting together a good stamp or postal-history collection. The second, possibly of more direct interest to the reader, puts the simple question as to how this general cost figure compares, on average, with that of a good topical/thematic collection.

The cost of setting up a collection depends on both philatelic and purely personal factors. Included are the type of collection—if it contains a preponderance of the early or the classical stamps the cost will be very much higher than if these expensive items are avoided in favour of the far more reasonably priced later issues—while the collection which includes a lot of popular varieties to the exclusion of cheaper stamps is a far more costly one to assemble than one which follows the catalogue to their exclusion. But the most important factor, and one which has a very considerable amount of control over all the others, undoubtedly is the money which the owner is prepared to make available for his collecting requirements.

Before comparing the cost of a thematic/topical type of collection with that of stamps or postal history, it would perhaps be a convenient point at which to dispose of two popular fallacies popular outside the stamp world.

The first fallacy is that a wonderful topical collection can be assembled at little or no cost and that this will provide the owner with an endless round of pleasure and enjoyment. This is, of course, utter nonsense. The second fallacy is that a collection made up from odd purchases of stamps and covers and assembled in a haphazard fashion can be thrown into the stamp market and will be snapped up, giving the owner a handsome profit. Never! It will be thrown from one dust heap to another. Knowledgeable collectors will surely need no further comment here on these two 'popular' and highly erroneous ideas.

It is a recognised fact that, in the case of the thematic collection, the expertise of the owner is the first requirement, with the money occupying second place. As a consequence, a very good subject/topical collection will cost the owner far less than a good stamp or postal-history collection. Here, of course, the term 'good' relates to two aspects: (a) the standing of the collection within its particular sphere; and (b) the amount of pleasure and satisfaction which it gives to the owner. It certainly does not relate to the eventual yield in terms of cash.

Who spends the most?

It seems to be a common supposition, at least in Great Britain, that to indulge extensively in competitive collecting is an expensive pastime. Is this true or false? In this connection an exercise was set up to see how the competitive and the non-competitive collectors in the thematic world compared as regards expenditure. A number of collectors were asked to quote their outlay on a year-by-year basis and to make a serious effort to arrive at real rather than guess-work figures. To ensure that the sample was as representative as possible, care was taken to include collectors in the first flush of enthusiasm as well as those who were more mature. By asking for figures on a yearly basis, it was possible to arrive at the total and annual costs of collecting, as well as the pattern of expenditure.

Two very interesting results emerged. The first was that the average annual expenditure of each of the competitive collectors was only slightly higher than that of the non-competitive collectors. This was surprising and at first a little difficult to accept. The other fact which came to light was that the pattern of expenditure of the competitive group of collectors differed considerably from that of the non-competitive. This difference in expenditure patterns helps to explain the first conclusion that there was little difference in the average annual amount spent on collecting by these two types of collector. It is this difference in pattern which is so interesting.

The competitive collector has to spend on the purchase of the top-quality material, the frame and postage fees as well as for insurance within a relatively short period. He also tends to concentrate his expenditure on quite a small part of the collection. Thus it becomes essential to budget for a peak of expenditure over a very short period. One or two of these collectors either had to stop collecting in other areas or sell material to meet all the costs of exhibiting. To many it was something in the nature of a once-only expenditure.

On the other hand, non-competitive collectors spread their expenditure much more evenly and, compared with the competitively minded enthusiast, as a continuous outlay rather than in one large lump. Very many non-competitive collectors in the sample had managed to build up quite large collections by the very easy method of using spare cash from their ordinary income. This was just a matter of it being 'easy and often'.

In the main, it is neither the total amount of cash nor the average amount which characterises the two types of collecting. It is the pattern of spending which counts.

Finance for the non-competitive collector

Because of the very wide area from which the material can be drawn, the non-competitive collector enjoys a considerable amount of latitude regarding the amount of money which must be spent to produce a good, attractive collection. Other than his pocket, there are no restrictions, high or low, on the cost of the stamps and other items for the collection.

At the top end of the scale, there are usually many stamps and covers to be found which would be considered expensive by most collecting standards. For example, the owner of a collection on the subject of ships would undoubtedly regard a cover or a document signed by Columbus as one of the highlights of the collection. If the stamp showing the famous *Lady McLeod* ship was also included in the collection then it would contain two of the gems of the collecting world. But they would be very expensive items. Much of the attraction of the collection would be its sparkle.

At the other end of the scale, the ATA Handbook No. 247, *Ships on Stamps*, gives a list of several thousands of stamps, all of which are good buys from the thematic point of view, and many are very reasonable in price as well. A collection which comprises stamps and other items drawn mainly from the inexpensive rather than the expensive part of the money scale will produce plenty of attraction and enjoyment solely because of the wide variety it contains.

It is important to notice that the choice of the subject which it is proposed to collect can affect expenditure to quite a surprising extent. There is a considerable amount of information, much of a thematic nature, in Chapter 1 which is also relative to the financial side of the hobby. At the risk of repetition, I emphasise that the number of reasonably priced items which can be found for a collection with a title which is restrictive and narrow in character is very small. This will drive the collector to increase expenditure by including more costly items. Alternatively, the collection can be downgraded by including stamps, etc., which are scarcely on the edge of the subject. But to do this usually results in a loss of attraction, pleasure and enjoyment from the collection. There is, then, a need to take money into account when choosing the topical/subject or theme which it is proposed to collect.

Very well, if a wide-open subject such as flowers or birds or children on stamps is the decision then presumably there will be no money worries? Not quite so fast please, good reader. If, as an absolute rule, only the very low cost material the cheaper covers are taken up and some better class stamps etc. are never included in the collection, there is a distinct possiblity of two sorts of risk. The first is that a high proportion of the everyday angles of the collection will be poorly displayed. The other likelihood is that, despite the very best efforts, the collection will seem to lack lustre and have a sameness bordering on the unattractive. The kind of rule which requires that only inexpensive stamps should be bought 'as a matter of principle' deserves to be broken every time that the needs of the collection require it. In other words, the collection comes first.

A collection calling

I am an abandoned collection! My owner no longer has the slightest interest in my welfare nor is it any compensation to me to know that this often happens to some collections. Very well, why not give me away? To this suggestion the owner rather unkindly passed the remark that he had not the audacity to do so, although he could see little use for it at the moment—and it might be valuable one day.

As positively the last resort, why don't you sell me? That also is not favoured for the very simple reason that I contain a large number of those 'stamps' which are currently produced by the owners of uninhabited islands or non-existent 'states' and which, therefore, have not the slightest need for any postal services whatsoever. Very often they fit quite nicely into the development of the subject/topical with a creditable representation of the birds, fishes, the flora of the territory in question. Some concern very popular motifs such as Christmas or Shakespeare. Although they are designated as 'stamps' they are more correctly seen as labels. Fine for collecting, but as such there is at present a considerable risk that they will be frowned upon when offered to many dealers. Rather than risk a refusal and a red face, the owner finds the highest shelf, the most out-of-sight spot, where he can leave the collection.

It is, of course, entirely consistent with the freedoms of collecting as to whether these labels-cum-stamps should be included in the collection or not. The author is quite prepared to express surprise, delight or sympathy, whichever is appropriate, when a collection containing lots of them is disposed of and the net sum realised is made known. He has a fairly good idea of the market value of his own collection if and when—and is quite happy to leave things at that.

Insurance
There is no doubt whatsoever that the least popular subject for collectors is insurance. It is not only unpopular, but it is unwanted and unpalatable to most of them. The author recently attended such a session billed to last a whole hour. It was given by a crinkly-faced old fellow, noted for his humour, and he used every possible device, including slides and audience participation and the lot to help to get it over. Despite all his efforts, about the usual number of the audience fell asleep. These notes will, therefore, be very brief.

Insurance can be effected for two purposes: to cover the transit to and from an exhibition or when the collection is in the owner's care at his residence. Whether the collection is insured or not for either of these purposes is the owner's prerogative. Signing the contract is easy, but it is when a claim comes to be made that the difficulties for the collector may start. Here's the picture.

You may lose a single stamp or more, up to the whole houseful of albums, stockbooks and all the miscellaneous material and are fully entitled to make a claim for this loss. Insurers are reasonable people and your contact with them will be easier and give better results if you can:

(a)   Show proof of ownership. It is of little value to plead that, now that it is lost, how can I prove that I had this stamp in my collection? Can you say precisely where and when you bought it and from whom? Also the cost? A copy of an auction catalogue with a bid figure in the margin proves nothing but the production of a photocopy of the auctioneer's receipt settles the matter. The best general line is to have a photocopy of each page in the collection, preferably made on a reduction-process machine to reduce the bulkiness of the records. One collector who lives very many miles from the nearest copying machine and who hates the sight of them finds it easier and quicker to make a small accurate drawing of each page and then to insert the vital insurance details on this. He also updates the sheet valuations on it so that he knows what to cover and claim. This covers the second point:

(b)   Give an authenticated purchase price and then the cost of replacing the item(s) today. Honesty and reasonableness are the keynotes here. Thus if an item was purchased at two-thirds catalogue a couple of years ago and you are now proposing to claim the greatly enhanced price of the full catalogue, then you must have a good reason for so doing.

Lastly, insurance contracts are made 'in the utmost faith' by both parties and you are one of them. If you effect an insurance for a sum arrived at by guess work rather than detailed calculation then you are guilty of pretence. Nor is this mitigated in any way if no claim is made, it is just that the act of indifferent faith has not come to light. The defence of over-insurance is very difficult, and under-insurance runs the risk of the proportionate loss adjustment rule. These and other aspects of insurance will be readily explained by the assurers if you take the trouble to enquire about them. But it is up to you to ask.

The finance of competitive collecting

The competitive collector, especially if he embarks on international exhibiting, finds that there is a need to have regard for two cost-equating factors: the condition of an item; the degree of scarcity of it. Both can contribute materially towards the cost of the better class of material which must be included in the entry if it is to secure a good award. The first of these, condition, invariably has a considerable effect on cost prices and the following practical suggestions are offered to the reader.

Try to get a sound working experience of what is meant by condition and how it can affect the buying price; the merit of your entry as seen by the judges in the exhibition; and—only if you feel so inclined—the selling figure.

The author considers the next suggestion is of particular importance to topical/thematic/subject collectors. In order to increase your personal thematic expertise, make as many dummy runs as possible in the art of balancing the cost of a stamp or other item against the amount of merit which it will bring to your collection. These dummy runs have nothing to do with buying, so you can arrive at the decision in complete isolation from other factors. On the one hand there is the price and this can either be seen in the dealer's stock or it is what you are prepared to bid for it in a sale. Your knowledge of condition will be useful here. Against this, do some thinking along the lines 'Where will it fit into the collection?' If you can visualise a place, you are then entitled to ask yourself the second question 'How much will it add to the story which is not there now? Will it add a bit of competitive "sparkle" to my entry or show a particular facet of the entry in a much better way than the item already in it?' Having measured the thematic worth of the stamp etc. all you have to decide is whether a purchase would be justified or not. Do not leave this exercise until you are faced with a 'yes or no' position over a dealer's stockbook or when the bidding is running against you, for unless you are blessed with a very stable temperament, the decision as to which is the greater, the cost or the worth, may well be disturbed by a multitude of intruding thoughts.

What about the money requirement of exhibiting? Most collectors strenuously resist making a budget, however commendable this may be. So why not call it a realistic forward picture of the cash angle? This accepted, then what do you get out of it, adding up the cost of the extra material which you think is needed, the cost of insurance and of high value postages, not forgetting the incidentals at 20 per cent for emergencies? Deciding to go into big exhibiting competitively, without that forward cost estimate, is about comparable with trying to sail a boat into a harbour mouth without a rudder. Both can be very worrying to the owner. Fine if all goes well, but what if it does not?

Listening to the experiences of other collectors shows that it is dangerous to guess the cost of insuring the entry against loss or damage to and from the point of the exhibition, so get competitive quotes against the sight of a completed proposal form. It is easy to leave this exercise until the eleventh hour, but it is likely that you will wish that you had worked this out more efficiently when faced with the option of whether to insure or not and time is already against you.

The cost of getting the entry to the point of the exhibition—and this may well be several thousands of miles away—will depend on whether you are to secure the services of the commissioner(s) for your country or not, and there is more about this elsewhere in the book.

Lastly, when considering the cost of giving the entry every possible chance of a good win by raising its thematic and philatelic content as high as you can, do drop the idea that the sky is the limit. In thematics this is not always so. Primarily, every facet of the story which the entry must tell must shine clearly and brightly. If rarity is one of the judging criteria, make every effort to secure that crystal-clear story of your theme or comprehensive coverage of your subject or topic by items which are difficult to find, rather than by everyday, easy-buy material.

5 Backwards and Forwards

The title of this chapter would undoubtedly be much easier to understand if it could be read as 'Looking backwards for a comparatively short space of time and going forward to effect a considerable amount of progress!' In other words, to make a brief recap of the coverage of the book up to this point and then to deal with the balance of the practical aspect of collecting in detail in so far as it concerns the thematic/topical/subject enthusiasts. This entails summarising the most important of the earlier thoughts and then their impact on the collecting; after that, to set the scene for the three chapters which follow. Why three chapters? For the very good reason that they make up the very core of thematic collecting—putting the collection together.

It would be both unwise and incorrect to assume that these three very practical parts will be of use to only the newcomer to thematics. Even if you have been an enthusiast for quite a while and the shape of your collection is now starting to emerge clearly, there may well be plenty of ideas in these three chapters which can be utilised, if not today, then very possibly tomorrow.

By far the most important aspect of this book is restated here so that it is given greater stress. It is that the objects of collecting are to secure pleasure, enjoyment, fun, satisfaction and relaxation for the collector. Sometimes too there are valuable educational aspects—of discovering rather than learning.

The previous chapters were concerned with some thoughts on three topics: first, the easy ideas and the definitions of the terms 'topical', 'thematic' and 'subject'; second, the advantage for the collector in having at least the basic knowledge of stamp collecting before going into thematics. After that the knowledge and practice of philately should be pursued as a parallel activity with thematic/topical/subject collecting. The third point was that the use to which the collection was to be put could make a considerable amount of difference as regards the type of material which should be included in the collection and the way in which it was presented.

It is hoped that by now the reader will have no particular difficulty in accepting that the words 'topical' and 'thematic' have both general and specific usages. Thus the broad term 'thematic', in Great Britain, also describes the thematic class in competitions and is made up of the theme and subject types of entry. In the USA and outside the sphere of internationals the terminology varies. In the broad sense the term 'topical' has an extremely wide usage, whilst 'thematics' is preferred by certain collectors. In the competitive area, events staged by the American Topical Association use the term 'topicals' whilst those run by the American Philatelic Society are judged by the regulations of the Inter-American Federation with theme and subject classes.

The value of a sound working knowledge of stamp collecting should not be underestimated. The better the collector's philatelic knowledge, the better the collection will be from the thematic merit and competitive viewpoints. There are two targets: thematics and stamp collecting.

On the third point, it is hoped that readers will not now be worried that the line between non-competitive and competitive collecting is not precise. But it should now be clear that competitions have high objectives and creditable awards, but at the price of the observance of certain disciplines. Non-competitive collecting allows the collector freedom. However, this requires the acceptance of certain risks and losing the way, thematic style, is surely one of these.

Now to look forwards. The primary objective of every collector is to establish the collection and thereafter to foster its growth along lines which will give him the greatest possible satisfaction. He may be aiming at just one or two albums to contain the complete topical/subject/thematic collection. Alternatively, nothing short of a whole row of albums covering every aspect of the subject will produce the pleasure and satisfaction that other collectors seem to need.

The basic steps towards this end—setting up the collection—are:

(a)   Select a suitable subject or topical or theme.

(b)   Visualise how the collection is to be put together and, if need be, formulate a plan. In short, get to grips with the precise method of collecting.

(c)   Secure the stamps, covers and other items, not forgetting the sheets and albums. Then do all the mounting and, lastly, apply the finishing touches in the writing-up.

These three basic steps, in order, are, therefore, the subjects of the next three chapters.

---

6   Making the Selection

This chapter concerns all collectors. It is designed to be of value to each, irrespective of whether a theme, topical or subject is in mind. It caters for both the enthusiast with a fairly clear idea of what the collection is going to be based on, as well as the 'clean-starter' who will have much more of an open mind about selection. Finally, the collector looking for a story-telling theme, capable of touching the imagination right from the start, will find a sizeable part of this chapter for his use and guidance.

Certain broad-band subjects, such as space, art, Americana and music contain so much stamp and other material that it is essential to restrict the collection to particular parts of the subject. It is therefore necessary for the process of selection to cover the decision as to which components of these types of collection are to be included and which give a very restricted coverage.

It may be true that there is nothing new under the sun but there is certainly no limit to the number and range of the topicals, themes and subjects from which the choice can be made. For initial reference purposes, it has been possible to list only a small percentage of these in Appendix A. The biggest storehouse for ideas and inspirations is the Bibliography.

From whichever angle you are approaching the job of making your selection, there is one point which must be fully appreciated. It is a very simple one. Just as collecting is a very pleasurable and satisfying activity, so making the selection is a real and enjoyable component of this pleasure.

On no account should this selection process be hurried. Why? This is for two very simple reasons: it is a part of your pleasure and the major factor which governs the shape and the progress of your collection. In fact, a recent broad-based survey showed that nearly 90 per cent of the unsuccessful collections were either hastily selected or chosen without a realistic idea of what was involved.

Right from the start

The very first thing to do is to find a subject, topical or theme which, in your hands, will be an unqualified success. To attain this you need:

1   To have complete confidence that the subject is right for you.

2   To make the right start.

3   To have a reasonably sound idea of where you are going. Many collectors start with very little idea about this and, for lack of a simple guide, are compelled to feel their way along until much later, when the collection is well under way. Then sometimes the whole exercise misfires. To be compelled to make big changes at a late stage is most unsatisfactory.

4   To find yourself with a collection which can be handled comfortably and enjoyed. This means that it must prove to be within the limits of your time, expertise and pocket. Of course, you are fully entitled to be somewhat extravagant, even adventurous, about the two first types of expenditure—time and expertise—because your ability is bound to increase as you go along. But perhaps it might be wise to be a little less extravagant with the third, the amount of money which you will be spending.

Here are suggestions for choosing the right subject.

STEP 1
Turn to the 'Short list of subjects' in the Appendix and read this over two or three times. Make a list of not less than six which seem to produce the most pleasant impressions. No other ideas matter at this stage. It is an exercise of the type 'I like this, I like that, but I really do like this next one more than any so far.' And so on.

STEP 2

With the subjects which you do not relish out of the way,
concentrate on the short list. Now the aim is to find the top
favourite and the runner-up. First strike out those remaining
which you fancy the least, then those which you like quite well,
but where you have no knowledge of the background of
the subject. By this time only two or three subjects should
remain.

Here is an example of these two steps—it was produced by a
very co-operative fellow passenger on a nice warm train during
a snowstorm!

Favoured from short list in Appendix	*Step 1*	*Step 2*
Art	Art (WB)	
Artists		
Christmas		
Composers		
Costume	Costume	Costume (runner-up)
Education		
Entertainment	Entertainment	Entertainment (top favourite)
Ethnology	Ethnology	
Famous people	Hats	
Hats but not hair		
Musical instruments		
Recreation	Recreation	
Theatre	Theatre	

Note that because all the subjects listed in the short list in the
Appendix can be developed into good collections, my fellow
passenger was therefore sure that by going for 'entertainment'
he was on quite firm ground for a good start.

If your firm choice comes out to be one of the wide-band
subjects (note that these are marked '(WB)' in the short list),
then you are very nearly home and dry. There is no doubt
whatsoever that any one of these subjects can easily be made
into an excellent and attractive collection. But this does not

mean that you can turn to Chapter 8 on collection building. You need a secondary selection process to help decide which components of the subject are to go into the collection in detail. This is covered later in this chapter.

What do you do if none of the items in the short list make the slightest appeal to you? The answer is very simple: make up a 'most-favoured list' on the lines of the example just given with the subjects in the order in which they come to mind. The application of the techniques for Step 1 and Step 2, plus a little imagination and enthusiasm, will nearly always single out your winner.

This routine is based on the single, simple criterion of what is liked the most. There are other very practical hurdles over which your top favourite and the runner-up must be tested. Happily you are now in the same position as very many other collectors in that you have a very good idea of what you would like to collect and all that is wanted is the finalisation. This is covered in the section which follows.

Have idea—needs finalising
It may well be that, during the reading to this point, a fairly clear idea of what you would like to collect has already begun to take shape and all you need is a little more information on what to take into account, so that the whole project can gel. It is certainly wise not to immediately spend your time, money and enthusiasm on what may well be no more than just a bright idea. So why not make a check that you are on the right lines from the very start?

First, collecting is synonymous with fun and pleasure so it is absolutely essential that your choice of what to collect gives you the very maximum yield. The first check is to make sure that collecting the subject which you are so keen about will be thoroughly enjoyable from start to finish. Of course, it may be equally important to you that it allows a bit of adventuring in the world of knowledge and understanding. If so, then it must be capable of satisfying your type of (thematic) exploring. Make a test of the real collecting capacity of your favourite idea in the following way. Think of all the ways it could be expanded and make a list of them. A few words about each will suffice for the time being. As each occurs to you it should be included in this list without worrying about any sort of order. Try to concentrate on finding every conceivable aspect of the subject. Do not hurry over this little job, nor worry about it either—time and yourself should be the best of friends. List A which follows will give you an idea what this random development process produced from the simple thought that it would be a good idea to collect everything about birds. The second part of this process is a contrast test which will help to get the situation into focus.

Next, look over List A of subjects and select your second favourite. Then, side by side with the first list, work out all the ways in which this second subject could be developed. Do a bit of cross fertilisation from one list to the other and it will surprise you how productive this can be. List B gives the expansion of the subject 'Flowers'. Notice that the appearance of 'flowers' as medicines and palliatives in List B generated the thought that birds can often provide domestic interest and relaxation. Hence the inclusion of 'Birds and man' as a late entry in List A. When it is certain that both lists have been fully developed, all is in readiness for the last step.

Contrast the thematic/subject/topical content of your most favoured list (List A) with that of the runner-up (List B). If they are roughly about the same amount, then your top favourite is the front runner for the final. Of course if List A is by far the wider (and more convincing) then there can be no argument that this subject is the one to go for. If the second (List B) contains substantially more, then weigh up the merits of each of these two subjects by contrasting the amount of enthusiasm which each generates in you.

Note that the yardstick to use includes (a) thematic content and (b) the amount of personal attraction.

List A	List B
The development of the	*The development of the*
subject 'Birds'	*subject 'Flowers'*
1 World distribution	Flowers of each country
2 Flight and migration	Flowers and insects
3 Food and feeding	Ceremony and flowers
4 Nesting	Propagation and seeding

5	Conservation	Protected flowers
6	Birds of my home town	Flowers of my home town
7	Birds and man	Herbs
8	Birds in heraldry	Flowers in heraldry

The following were added to the bird list by comparison with the flower list

9	Dangerous birds	Poisonous flowers
10	Birds and costume	Flowers and costume
11	Cage birds	Indoor flowers
12	Extinct birds	Ancient flowers

The following were added to both List A and List B as the result of item 12

13	Symbolic birds	Symbolic flowers
14	Birds on paintings	Flowers in paintings
15	Bird letter carriers	Flowers of message

As the result of spontaneous transference of items from List B to List A, and the parallel application of items 13 to 15, it has been possible to increase the range of the bird collection from 8 sections to 15. This growth will not necessarily increase the size of the collection in this proportion. It does, however, considerably increase the range and hence the attractiveness of the collection. In practice each list would run consecutively and the spacing shown above is for explanatory purposes only. A longer list of the section of the 'Bird' collection is given in the Appendix.

A word of warning: do not throw away the list of the subject which is now the 'tops' for you because it will be of considerable use to you later on.

Now, having found the firm favourite, comes that vital decision. It must clear the last hurdle, which is quite a practical one. This is that it must reasonably well pass the test that there will be sufficient stamps, covers and the like to allow a workable collection to be brought into being. In other words, is it viable? Will it turn out to be what you really wanted? Note that there are plenty of very attractive titles, but for which it is not possible to find enough stamps, covers etc. to complete about a dozen or so pages. There are a number of subjects such as 'Space' or 'Ships', not omitting 'Music' or 'Humanity', which are so wide that a whole lifetime would be needed to obtain a reasonably complete collection. So, get a fair idea in your mind's eye of the size of collection you think will suit you. Do you have enough time to tackle an extremely wide subject which will require a lot of your spare moments over a very long period? Or must it be a subject which can be picked up and put down at random and call for the minimum expenditure of your time? In between these two extremes there are literally hundreds of subjects which need an average amount of time and patience in order to produce a first-class collection. This question of the size of the collection is best measured first of all in terms of the time you need to spend on it. Here is an example of a 'not too big and not too short' type of collection. The figures were obtained from the check list of this subject, 'Ships on Stamps', and the collection arranged for non-competitive use and enjoyment. A useful working aim for this type of collection is about eight stamps per page.

Estimating the final size of the collection
Example: A subject collection of 'Ships on Stamps'

1 Number of stamps issued to date and considered essential for inclusion in the collection   646

FOR A NON-COMPETITIVE COLLECTION
2 Number of sheets needed for stamps (average 8 per sheet) = $\frac{646}{8}$ 80

3 Number of sheets required for all other types of items (estimated)   40

4 Total number of sheets needed today   120

5 Allowance for growth (estimated) (Note, this is a popular subject with the issuing administrations)   70

6 Size of the collection (ultimate) allowing 40 sheets per album for the 190 sheets   5 albums

FOR A COMPETITIVE COLLECTION
It is envisaged that the collection will be set up on a well-spaced, well-balanced standard throughout to meet the usual competitive style. Only a very limited amount of non-stamp material will be included. Particular care will be taken about the inclusion of any collateral-type items. (If need be, refer back to the section on the combined effect of size and colour which is on page 57.)

7	Number of stamps in the collection as issued to date (see item 1)	646
8	Number of sheets needed for the stamps at an average of 4.5 per sheet	144
9	Number of sheets wanted for other types of item	20
10	Total number of sheets required today	164
11	Estimated allowance for growth	24
12	Total number of sheets in the collection	188
13	Size of the collection	4 albums

(Note: albums can hold more sheets because of the exclusion of the bulky covers etc. Allow 50–55 sheets per album.)

The four albums contain about 200 sheets with a few specially prepared sheets for individual competitions. At this size, an entry for one of the major competition events is quite a reasonable proposition. For internationals, it is considered that no difficulty would arise in filling at least the five minimum frames. For competitions on a lower level it should be possible to draw the material from any part of the collection and use this for an entry.

The author's non-competitive collection
The author has a massive appetite for material and he would include everything possible with a reasonable percentage of collateral material. On the other hand, the competitive standard of presentation, with an overall average of 4 stamps per page, has been rigorously maintained. The inclusion of a high proportion of non-stamp items at very generous spacings has the effect of increasing the size of the collection very considerably. Here is the estimated size.

14 Number of stamps issued to date (as before)   646
15 Sheets wanted for these stamps (average 4 per sheet) 160
16 Number of sheets for all other items   200
17 Allowance for future growth (estimated)   150
18 Total number of sheets in the collection   510
19 Size of the collection   13 albums
(Allow 40 sheets per album for bulky items)

Readers may wish to see the effect of the three standards (a non-competitive collection at close spacing between items, a competitive collection and the author's personal collection) on the size of the collection for sheets. Here are the figures from this example:

Collection	*Type*	*Sheets*	
		Now	*Future*
A	Non-competitive	120	190
B	Strictly competitive	164	188
C	All types of item included, but at competitive spacing standards	360	510

See also the size of the collection (*Illustration 6.1*).

Comments

1 Collectors are invariably very sensible folk and there should be no difficulty therefore in appreciating that, with the exception of the number of stamps issued to date (646), the figures are based entirely on the author's experience.

2 The job of finding the figures and arriving at sizes is a worthwhile and interesting exercise. Why not try a few examples for yourself?

Selecting a theme
Most owners of well-established theme collections, when specifically asked about it, insisted that there was no question of a need to sit down and make a selection as such. The choice was very much a 'natural' one and this particular aspect of setting up the collection gave rise to no real difficulties. Further they offered the information that the subject to which the theme was

directly related was the one which they much preferred above all others. It was also considered to be a very real advantage to have a sound understanding of the background to the subject, as well as a good knowledge of the details of a number of its component parts.

Especially for the intending collector, it is most important that the value of making a good selection of the theme to be collected, and of securing the logical progression of its story, should not be underestimated. In order to set up a successful collection you need to have the advantage of the following:

1   A clear liking for the subject on which the theme is to be based.

2   A sound and up-to-date knowledge of the basis of that subject.

3   A detailed knowledge of most of the component parts of that subject, either now or subsequently acquired.

To these three must be added a fourth and very important requirement:

4   The ability to discern the steps in the logical development of this basic subject, despite the fact that the information may have to be drawn from a number of sources. Also, it is essential to be able to visualise how these steps can be reproduced in stamps, covers and the like, within the pages of the collection.

When these four objectives have been adequately secured, the rest of the work of setting up the collection is quite easy. Of course, not every one possesses the ability to recognise the steps and their order, first in the subject and then to translate them into the story of the theme. So, if you are not strong in this particular area, tread rather warily if the start on a theme collection is in mind. Why not explore the possibilities of setting up a subject-cum-theme type of collection? This could well be more to your liking.

If on the other hand, to be the happy owner of good and satisfactory theme collection is a 'must' for you, it is essential that, before the start is made, you should come to fair and honest terms with at least three of those four basic requirements given earlier. Measure your ability (and the success of the collection) against the following criteria:

1 That you are fully prepared to locate a subject for which you have a particular liking and that you will enjoy developing. The routine suggested earlier in this chapter for the selection of a subject can be followed for this purpose.

2 That you have the time, inclination and ability to conduct sufficient research into the basics of the subject (in the general sense) so that a comprehensive list of the component parts may be constructed. This means digging and delving into as many sources of information as possible, cross-checking them and finally arranging your list of sections of the whole in a reasonable order.

3 That you already enjoy having a flair for working out, in general terms, how the sources of information which you have consulted are arranged in sequences. Also that you are able to extract the core of information from each facet. Further, that you will be able to visualise and set up similar sequences using pages of stamps, covers etc.

In other words, if you like discovering information, as well as the correct order in which it should be presented, the theme collection is certainly for you. If, on the other hand, you must have the information all clearly worked out for you before it 'means a thing', then getting the best out of a theme collection will certainly mean a lot of hard work and very possibly some disappointments for you.

To start work on the collection before being sure that you are fully equipped, as regards these three criteria, does not necessarily mean that the project is bound to fail. There is a real risk, however, that because of the magnitude and complexity of the task of sorting out the details and getting the thematic story right, your enthusiasm may begin to fade somewhat. Then, as likely as not, the whole programme of collecting will peter out. If accepting challenges and taking risks bring sparkle to your enthusiasm, then go right ahead. But don't forget that it will mean a lot of hard work.

Perhaps you will feel inclined to ask why having a good detailed knowledge of the subject was not included in the list of the first essentials? This omission was for a very good purpose. It makes the point that, if a sound knowledge of the basis of a subject is already held, plus that of some of the details, then expanding into other parts of the subject is quite easy. It is axiomatic, however, that the better the knowledge of those parts of the subject covered in the collection the more extensive and valuable (thematically) it will become.

Here is a simple example showing how a single thought of a very general character can produce a satisfactory line of action for the individual.

The thought comes to mind that an interesting theme collection could be based on the rise and fall of famous people. Written in this way, the subject has the benefit of being very wide with plenty of lattitude for the expression of personal ideas. Also, as there are many stamps of famous people, getting the material for the collection should present no problem. But this latter, the great amount of material which can be secured, brings a special point to light. With so many stamps on this subject, it is essential that the collection must be restricted to only a part of it. Which part? Here the personal angle comes into play. Thus the author enjoys subjects which are of a scientific and mechanical nature, rather than of historical or sociological character. His collection would therefore cover only the famous scientists of the world. A short check shows that there are enough stamps and covers available at the moment to allow a good one-volume thematic collection to be set up. Fine. The last question undoubtedly is about the title to the theme. A short, apt and attractive one such as 'The Lives of Some Famous Scientists' seems to fill the bill; moreover, it is not over eye-catching and it directly indicates the purpose of the theme.

Now for the practical application of the ideas set out in this section of the chapter. It shows the nine practical steps which will allow a basic thought to be developed into a working theme collection.

From subject to theme in nine steps

Thematic area

Step 1 Select the basic subject from the short list or the Bibliography. (Use the routine suggested earlier) ⟶

General knowledge of subject

⟶ *Step 2* List the primary divisions of the total range of knowledge of subject ↓

Step 3 Select those primary divisions which appeal to you and can easily be made into a step in the thematic story ↓

Step 4 Re-arrange the selected primary divisions into a logical order to give the

Step 5 Write a brief description of each division of the story ↓

⟵ clearest story to your theme

The collection

Step 6 Expand the descriptions in Step 5 into the steps which each one requires to become a part of the collection ↑

⟶ *Step 7* Construct the collection. (Use Chapters 7 and 8 for guidance)

Step 8 Draft and write the introduction using Step 6 and the collection as guides ↑

For completion
Assemble the title, introduction and the collection. Check that the story of the theme is told in logical order

Step 9 Select a short and appropriate title. (Use Step 8 as a guide)

Note: The order in which these steps are taken, especially 8 and 9, is important because they can contribute considerably towards the success of the assembly of the collection. Readers who prefer a pictorial type of presentation will find *Illustration 6.2* of help.

For the subject collector
The simple steps by which the subject (generic type) can be developed to the subject (thematic type) are very similar to those just described for the production of a theme collection. In the subject collection, the order in which parts are presented in the make-up of the whole collection relates to the natural sequence of the basic subject itself. Sometimes this is a chronological one, or an accepted arrangement of families, classes and species. On many occasions the best order of the parts of the collection is that which produces the best picture of the owner's interest in the subject generally.

When using the nine steps just described Step 4 should be read as:

Step 4 Rearrange the selected primary divisions into the order which best illustrates the nature and purpose of the subject.

It is recommended that the intending subject collector should construct the equivalent of the nine steps given previously and make a particular point of choosing the terminology for it which fits his collection and subject the best. Further help with the listing of the component parts of the subject can be obtained from the example in the Appendix, which shows the complete breakdown of a well-established collection on birds. The owner is a lady with strong and active ornithological interests.

DESCRIBING THE COLLECTION
In both cases, the selection of a subject and of a theme as recommended in this chapter will produce a list of the divisions of the collection. This list has several very useful functions.

First it provides a verbal and mental picture of the parts of the collection. At first, this may well be an incomplete and rather illogical portrayal of the whole concept. As further parts suggest themselves, they should be added to the list. It is surprising how often new ideas about the completeness and the clarity of the thematic story will come to you. The place for these useful ideas is, of course, in the list.

Second, when the list is considered to be reasonably well complete—and this may not be until long after the work on the

Example of the difference in the meaning of the term "Cachet" as used in Great Britain and the United States of America

Cachet
(U.S.A. terminology)

Cachet
(British terminology)

1.1 The two meanings of the term 'cachet'

Transits of Venus

These events are quite rare. They occur in pairs separated by an interval of eight years, but these pairs are separated by more than a century. Expeditions are formed to observe the transits.

TRANSIT OF VENUS, 1882 DEC. 6.
U. S. EXPEDITION TO CAPE OF GOOD HOPE.

Professor O. C. Marsh
New Haven
Connecticut
U.S.A.

Cover carried on the Transit of Venus Expedition, 1882.

The other transit of this pair was on 9th December 1874.
The next pairs will occur in 2004 and 2012.

1.2 A good postal history item

Symbolic trees   Rep: of S. Africa

"Steadfastly Strong"

Dr. Hendrick Frensch Verwoerd.

P.M of Rep: of S.A. from 31.5.1961

Died. 6ᵗʰ Sept. 1966

2.1 An item clearly relevant to the tree collection

2.2 Relevant to the symbolic section of the tree collection

I. R. SALE
36, BROUGHTON RD.,
W. EALING, W.13.

2.3 Not relevant to the tree collection but suitable for Art or religion on stamps

2.4 Included on personal grounds but not those of thematic merit

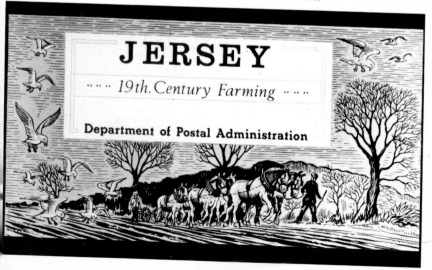

The birds of the West Indies   Grenada Grenadines.

Northern ring necked
plover.

Long billed
Curlew

Snowy Egret.

Black bellied tree duck

Purple Martin

2.5 Enforced attraction to the central item

"TREE & MANKIND" COLLECTION   WOODEN IMPLEMENTS

EXPLANATORY SHEET

THE LARGE DARK SHEET COMPELS ATTENTION

2.6 Defective visual impact

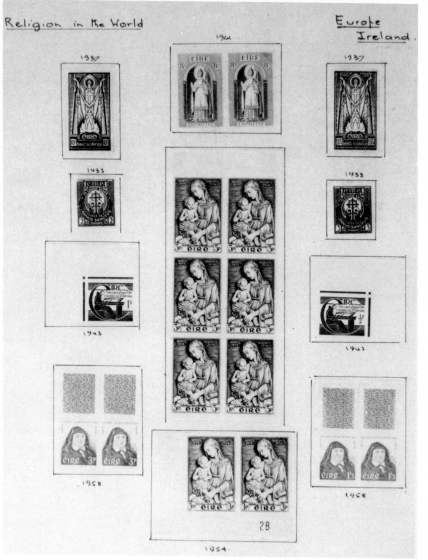

2.7 Example of an overcrowded sheet

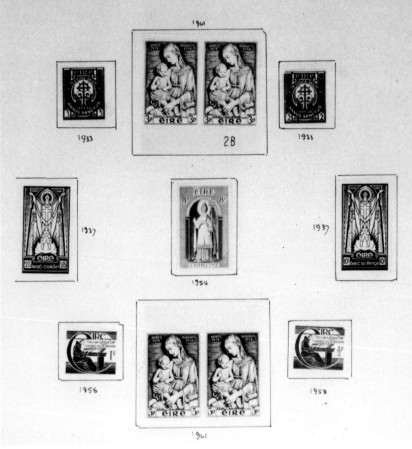

2.8 Improved spacing of the overcrowded sheet

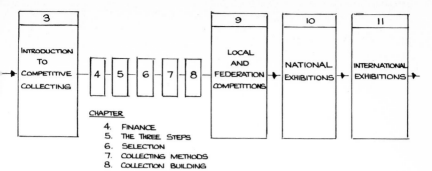

3.1 The chapter sequence for competitive collecting

3.2 'I thought that I had a stamp with a bird on it somewhere'

TYPE OF COLLECTION	BOOK REF.	SIZE OF THE COLLECTION (ALBUMS)
NON-COMPETITIVE (BUT RESTRICTED RANGE OF MATERIAL)	A	1 2 3 4 5
COMPETITIVE	B	1 2 3 4
NON-COMPETITIVE WITH "IN DEPTH" COVERAGE	C	1 2 3 4 5 6 7 8 9 10 11 12 13

.1 How the type of collection affects the size

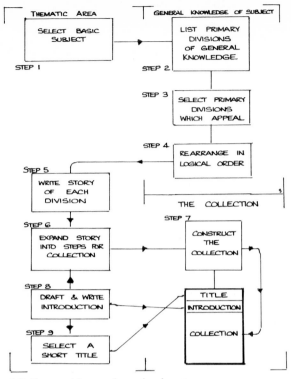

6.2 From subject to theme in nine steps

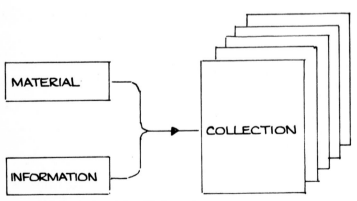

7.1 Both material and information are
required for the collection

collection has been under way for some time—you are well prepared to move to the next stage. This is to rearrange the whole of the list so that it will produce a series of logical pictures in the collection. Try to visualise how each step is likely to appear on the sheets and make a point of working out how one section will lead into the following section. Step 5 in the nine steps from a subject to a theme will give a starting point for this process. A word of advice—keep this revised list handy because it is the key to the development of the collection.

THE NEED FOR AN INTRODUCTION

Because this section about the need for an introduction occurs at the very end of the chapter, it does not mean that it is a minor requirement for the make-up of a good collection. On the contrary, and especially in the competitve world, it is quite an important item. The form and function of the introductory sheet of a competition entry will be covered in Chapters 9–10.

Broadly speaking, the non-competitive collector can put whatever he wishes on the title sheet of his album. But there are two points which perhaps ought to be taken into account by a discerning collector.

Thematic, that is topical, subject or theme, collections differ from the traditional stamp collections in that they do not follow any catalogue sequence. Also each section of the collection grows at its own pace, depending on what items are spotted by the owner on offer and purchased. This means that the sheets of the collection are thumbed over quite frequently to introduce new material, rearrange it or even look over it for the sake of pure enjoyment. It suggests that the provision of a reference showing both what material there is and where it is situated can make a realistic saving on the wear and tear on the sheets and the albums as well. Not only is there a saving on the albums but also in the time and temper of the owner. What better reason is there for an introduction which will give the owner a guide to the contents of the collection?

Although collecting is a personal activity there is a decided tendency for the collection to take on a rather stereotyped style and so fail to reflect the character of the owner. The author suggests that a short paragraph at the start of the introduction could do much to restore a personal touch to the collection.

7 Collecting Methods

Perhaps a little, perhaps a lot
The reader may suppose that this heading might mean that a little thought about the setting-up of the collection could result in a lot of fun and pleasure. That is certainly very true, but there is another idea behind this particular phrase. It concerns the small matter of arriving at a good balance between your way of thinking about how to get the collection together and what the subject or theme demands in real practice.

The assembly of a good collection nearly always requires at least some amount of thought. How much depends upon such factors as the type of collection and the depth to which you propose to take it. In fact it is very often the collection and not the collector which dictates how involved it ultimately becomes. Some types of collection require only a very small amount of serious thought to be put together very creditably whilst others, especially themes, call for a fair amount of detailed planning, both before and during the work of assembly. Let's add up all the bits of planning which are usually needed. First there are the thoughts about the selection of the most suitable topical/subject/theme. Next will be the question of which stamps will best fit into the several parts of the collection, then the order in which they should be mounted to tell the story nicely. Last come the very practical details of where to purchase the items required. Subject for subject, topical for topical and theme for theme, these little bits of thinking can add up to the need for 'perhaps a little planning, perhaps a lot'.

Behind this need for just the right amount of planning (and no more) lies the linkage with the pleasure, satisfaction and enjoyment which can result. It is therefore quite reasonable to think that the amount of pleasure which each collector finds to his liking will vary quite widely from one to another. Some consider that it is unnecessary to make even an outline plan whilst others are firmly convinced that everything, including collecting, must start with a plan of some kind. How do each of these fare with regard to their collecting activity?

Perhaps you are sure that the most enjoyable way of starting the collection, as well as running it, is literally to throw all the material together into a random heap and then have a grand sort out. Well, if you are quite positive about it, then that's fine, because it is your way of getting pleasure and satisfaction. Even so, there is little doubt that you should never allow yourself to embark upon a type of collection which can demand a lot of time and thought to be planned satisfactorily. There are, in fact, a large number of subject/topical collections which, from start to finish and providing that they are not explored too deeply, call for only a minimal amount of easy planning.

On the other hand, perhaps your make-up has an inbuilt liking for planning. Others may see this as being excessively methodical but you recognise it as nothing more than good, sound common sense. If so, then a theme of your choosing, with a well-constructed plan and based on a clear logical development, will undoubtedly give a lot of pleasure and satisfaction. Of course, the initial progress will not be very startling; also, quite a long time may elapse before the collection begins to take a recognisable shape. But that's no particular worry because it is very usual.

Whichever way you prefer to tackle the job of setting-up and running the collection, one thing is quite certain. You will always have the pleasure of recognising the pattern of your collection because it is the visible end product of your planning; perhaps it requires a little, perhaps a lot.

Clearing a clutter

'Yes, these two stamps are precisely what I have been looking for. I an lucky to have found them at last. They will fit nicely into the collection just here, but it's certainly a nuisance that this means the redesign of two or even three of the sheets. I certainly have not the time to do all that right now, so I will put them between these two sheets of the album and then I will know exactly where they are later on.'

'This cover is a beauty. It's going to be a real asset to my topical collection because it opens up an angle which hadn't occured to me until I saw it on sale today. Mind you, it will need some other material, possibly a couple of stamps, to go with it to set it off nicely. For the time being I'll put it on my desk until I can spot the stamps. Not out of sight because I don't like leaving these things too long. I am sure to get around to doing the job soon—not tomorrow, but I am bound to be free next week—another day—some day.'

No, this is not going to be a moralising lesson saying 'Do it now or else.' This chapter is a practical way of tackling some of the very usual and very irritating experiences of the majority of collectors.

Collectors are enthusiastic and busy people. They enjoy finding and buying the material for their collections and the more of it the better. Doing this is just as interesting as the actual job of mounting it up for inclusion in the albums. In this connection, the owner of a topical/thematic/subject collection has a rather different situation to cope with from that of the average stamp collector. Granted that no collector is lucky enough to get the stamps, etc., precisely at the right moment but there is an additional point that each section of a thematic collection continues to grow as a separate entity. In the case of the conventional collection, the bulk of the growth occurs at one point and this is usually both easy and convenient to locate. The thematic collection is therefore likely to be handled rather more than the conventional one. This frequent turning to and fro not only gives rise to excessive wear and tear on the contents but also disturbs any loose items. Treatment like this is certainly not good for the collection or the condition of the contents.

Another point is that a certain amount of background information is usually required before each page can be completed. This calls for some degree of research, possibly elsewhere; further, this research should be completed before the mounting-up is started. During the time that this is being done what happens to the stamps, covers, etc. awaiting mounting?

For these and other reasons it is very rare therefore that purchases can be taken home and mounted up immediately and nearly always there are some ancillary jobs to be done before even one new item is incorporated into the collection. The stamps, covers, cancellations, FDCs and the odd miniature sheet undoubtedly have to be put somewhere. Too often it is the not-thought-out place, the easy way out of dropping them all into the album at some point near where they are to go ultimately. Too soon it is a case of having a collection plus a clutter. Clearing one clutter can be very expensive in time and temper. To have to clear more than one could quite well be disastrous! The main function of this chapter is to describe a simple system which can be easily set up and is specifically designed to help avoid the difficulties and irritations which have just been described.

The basis of the system
The system suggested here is based on two simple concepts. The first is that the fewer times the material is handled, the better. The other fundamental is quite different. Nicely stated, it is that all unmounted material, information and the like should be located into a flow line towards the collection. In more general usage, it means 'Don't lump the material into a pile to await the time when it can be dealt with. Sort it out right at the start and put it into the quickest and best pathway into the collection.'

Would you take the trouble to join a Society for the Protection of Pleasure and Enjoyment? Maybe, but if there were no fees (or dues), no entrance forms to be filled out, no semi-official meetings to attend and yet, if the sole aim of the society was to ensure that you never received less than your rightful share of pleasure and enjoyment, you very likely would enrol without delay. Of course you would. Then that is precisely the object of this system, to ensure that your material gets into the collection with the minimum of delay and at the same time you obtain the full measure of fun, pleasure and enjoyment from the collection. The particular pleasures of thematics spring from the inspirations and ideas produced by looking at the pages of the collection, the enjoyment grows as the sheets are completed and the story that they are telling unfolds. Without doubt, to see more and more of a theme developing or aspects of a subject coming into the picture is the 'tops' in satisfaction. But if these happy processes are punctured every time the albums are opened by showers of loose stamps, covers and like, then away goes the very best part of the enjoyment. It is so easy to have your pleasure spoiled by the sight of a heap of material awaiting this or that job to be done. Not only does this situation prevent the full enjoyment of the collection, but it also stops the full appreciation of its good qualities. Each time that it becomes necessary to explain away unfinished sheets or to apologise for a floating population of loose material, there is a loss of fun, pleasure, enjoyment and satisfaction. Even an experienced collector suffers considerable annoyance on being subject to interruptions of this sort. The system which is suggested here not only avoids these troublesome conditions but also does much to speed the progress of collecting. So why not support the Society for the Protection of Pleasure whose main plank is the adoption of this system?

There are only two rules to be observed. These are:

Rule 1

The collection proper should contain only those album sheets which are complete in every detail. That is, each sheet should be in apple-pie order with all the items required properly mounted and the writing-up, in the usual style of the collection, duly completed. The author takes the liberty of pressing the point that each sheet should be finished completely before it is put into the collection. This requirement is considered to be paramount, absolute and final. If the reader can think of any other ways of saying that it is 'must', then they should be included here too! The system described here provides an easy and safe place for holding all partially completed sheets until they are ready for inclusion in the collection.

Rule 2

That no loose item, whether it be a valuable stamp, a commercial cover or a like item, as well as any notes and information to be used ultimately in the collection should be without a duly recognised place away from the collection.

It is hoped that, in this rather long form, it will please

the collectors who enjoy definitions of an academic type. If, on the other hand, it seems to be disastously long and involved, then matters can easily be put to rights. For light relief try *Illustration 3.2*. Next make good use of the picture-book explanation which follows.

What every album sheet must have

The two essentials which must be ready on hand to allow an album page to be completed are: (a) the full complement of stamps, covers and the like items. In short, you must have all the material for the job. Also you must have (b) sufficient information to allow you to write up the whole sheet. Now add the MATERIAL and the INFORMATION and use them for the COLLECTION, as in *Illustration 7.1*.

The basic route into the collection

Illustration 7.2 shows a simplified route to get the material and the information into the form in which they will appear in the collection.

This is the basic sequence. (Note that the significance and the importance of the trial layout are explained later in this chapter).

HOW TO USE THE BASIC SEQUENCE

Here are three examples showing how this basic sequence can be used. They are: the easy day; when you have all the material but not all the information; and all the information but not all the material.

The easy day

There are no problems on those rare occasions when all the material and the information for a sheet (or group of sheets) come together at one and the same time. When this does occur it is wise to make every effort to complete the whole job as shown in the basic sequence without delay. For the thematic collector this kind of experience is far from being an every day event and the opportunity to make a direct addition to the collection is far too good to be lost.

When you have all the material available but not all the information

This is one of the more usual conditions. Very often only a very small but vital piece of information is wanted and is holding up the completion of a sheet or even a group of sheets. Sometimes that essential bit of information will suddenly come to light and at a time when it is least expected. To light on a key detail and to be able to fit it in at once is most pleasing even if it has taken a year or so to locate.

As additional information comes to light, it must be added to that already on hand and the whole carefully associated with the stamps, cover, etc., to which it refers. In this way a check can be made quite easily as to whether sufficient information has yet been found to allow the mounting-up process to be started. An occasional check of the material against the information serves to strengthen the focus of both as well as refresh the memory as to what is wanted in each case. This close association of the material and the growing file of notes and information is an important part of successful thematic collecting.

The precise form of the waiting information store is not important. The points which matter are: that it should be easy to handle; that it is clearly labelled on the 'facing front' surface; and that it is in such a place that it cannot escape the eye.

The author uses a stout, purpose-made cardboard box measuring 35cm x 30cm x 10cm, with a deep slip-over top, as his waiting information storepoint. With these dimensions all but the outsized sheets can be easily accommodated. *Illustration 7.3* will show how it is used.

Action: when all the information is complete use the basic sequence without delay

The order in which the papers etc. are placed within the waiting information store is a matter of personal preference. One way which avoids the 'last in and first out' order is to place the contents of the store in the approximate sequence in which it is expected that the balance of the information needed is likely to come to light. In this way, the amount of time required to find a particular item in the store, as well as the amount of handling, are cut to a minimum.

When you have all the information available but not all the material
This condition can be catered for by an arrangement on the lines of the previous one. It only requires the setting up of a

simple waiting material store which can be used as shown in
Illustration 7.4.

*Action: when all the material has been obtained use the basic
sequence without delay.*

THE HALF-AND-HALF CONDITION
In practice, and especially when beginning collecting a
particular subject, theme or topical, the condition most usually
encountered is one in which both more material and more
information are required. No problems arise from this kind of
situation nor is there a need for a third storage point. Unless the
functions of one of the stores is more applicable (in any
particular case) than the other, then it is a matter of the choice of
the collector as to which is used. The author has a good memory
and therefore prefers not to indulge in transferring items from
one box to the other unless there are strong reasons for so doing.
The borderline cases can be stored in either box of course.
Common sense dictates quite easily as to where the balance
should be placed.

WHY TWO SEPARATE STORES?
This is a very good question and one to which there is an
excellent answer based on purely practical reasons. First, the
life of many collections is surprisingly long and it is therefore far
better to have too much space than too little. Next, and possibly
of the greatest benefit, is the fact that each store is limited to one
function only. That is, one store directs attention to material
and the other to information and this helps considerably when
searching through them. To this must be coupled the
undoubted blessing of this system: all the unmounted stamps,
covers etc. must be in one of two places *and nowhere else.*

A SYSTEM SPRINGBOARD
The system described in this chapter rationalises the method of
getting the material and the information into the collection so
that it is easy, efficient and safe to operate. The basic
requirement is that it provides a positive route towards the
collection for all the types of item, information and data.
     To stow stamps etc. between the sheets of the collection

'until another day' is a negative-flow system. It is based on the idea of 'I do not know where to put this stamp or that reference at the moment so it must go somewhere.' Of course, if you particularly like negatives (and there are plenty of people who do) then by all means enjoy yourself in that way.

If, on the other hand, you are attracted to positive situations and conditions then why not enjoy using the ideas in this chapter about the two types of store as the springboard for your own ideas? You may well be very pleased with the results.

The trial layout

Especially when trying to find the best layout for a number of items of differing sizes, you may well need to make more than one trial layout and to contrast the advantages and disadvantages of each when they are side by side. The more different the shapes and the more strongly contrasting the colours, the more difficult it is to achieve a good layout. If you are a non-competitive collector, adopt the layout which gives you the greatest pleasure on a general inspection and at the same time tells the story of the theme or satisfies the correct and natural arrangement of the subject of topical.

The competitive collector will need to take plenty of time to experiment with layouts so that both general impression and logical development are shown in the best possible light. There is a need to make a study of the art of good presentation and help in this direction is given in the section of this book on competitive collecting.

There is now no further restraint on the pleasant business of building the collection and that is precisely what the next chapter is about.

8 Collection Building

In Chapter 1 emphasis was placed on the need for the thematic collector to think through the idea that a good knowledge of stamp collecting, both in respect of terminology and the practical work, would undoubtedly be very beneficial. To allow the starter collector to get off the ground satisfactorily, he was offered a short list of terms and skills and the second stage covered all that an advanced collector might need. It was left to the choice of the individual to settle the precise way in which the stamp collecting and the thematic collecting activities were to be integrated so that the net result was to the greatest advantage. In this connection, the *Illustration 8.1*, 'Your Route to Thematics', gives an overall picture of a progressive plan and which may be of use to readers.

It is in the building of the collection, and this is the object of this chapter, that the knowledge and skills of stamp collecting are of such direct and invaluable use. The degree to which they are applied throughout the building of the collection is clearly reflected in the quality of the end product: the sheets within the album covers. Generally, the integrated programme of stamp and thematic collecting results in widening the perspective and this brings with it a bonus in the shape of increased attractiveness in the range and style of the collection. These are particularly noticeable in the non-competitive area, where the collector is free to explore whatever angle he chooses. In the competitive area of collecting, the degree to which philatelic knowledge and skill should be in evidence depends largely on the level of the competition.

Moving from one level up to another undoubtedly brings the possibility of securing a better award, but it ought not to be overlooked that it also calls for a substantial increase in philatelic skill. Apart from awards, the happiest product of competitive collecting is unquestionably the satisfaction which comes from having prepared and submitted a credit-worthy entry. Along with this matter of an integrated programme of stamp collecting and thematics, which is so advantageous, the author considers that, because collecting is such a strongly personal activity, both he and the reader have certain responsibilities. It is the author's job to see that the collector finds sufficient information in this book and the reader must accept the responsibility for securing all the philatelic knowledge and skill required.

The Bibliography includes a number of general references to stamp collecting. Two of these, both by Charles E. Foster and with the titles of *How to Prepare Stamp Exhibits* and *Showcasing Your Collection*, will be found of very considerable help in both the practical and the background work of stamp collecting. It is of note that the function of this book and especially of this chapter is to extend the information given in the many works already published on stamp collecting so that the needs of the many topical/thematic/subject collectors are catered for fully and completely.

This is an Anglo-American book and accordingly looks after both sides of that thematic 'alliance'. The two excellent books by Charles E. Foster were written for American collectors and have a strong emphasis away from the use of sheets which are already fully printed and written up towards a 'do-it-yourself' type on quadrillé lined paper.

There are two points of interest. The layouts and procedures described in these two books are designed in conjunction with the requirements of each particular page as and when the collector comes to need it. These are precisely the same as those for the thematic collector, so these works are admirably suited for thematic/topical/subject collecting. No attempt will therefore be made to restate or duplicate the advice about layouts, except where the problems of the combination of size and colour occur. These are likely to be quite frequent events for the thematic collector and the solutions for a few examples are given for guidance in the section on 'this problem page' in Chapter 2, page 58.

The other interesting angle is that in Great Britain the use of quadrillé lined paper (the do-it-yourself paper of America) is quite usual for general stamp collecting and the need for converting the collector to this type does not therefore arise. Nevertheless, the information given in the two books previously quoted, in essence, is excellent and well recommended for use, not only in Great Britain but in Europe as well. It should be noted that there are signs that the advanced collector, especially in the competitive area of collecting in Great Britain, is leaning towards the use of an 'all-over' plain, high-white type of thin card for his entries. Although this requires a lot more care and patience at the sheet layout stage, it is claimed that it has the advantage of increasing the amount of contrast between the stamps and the surface of the sheet on which they are mounted. This helps to improve the general impression of the entry.

It is of further interest that the attractive 'picture border' type of sheet used in the US is almost unknown in Great Britain in any area of collecting. There is evidence that some collectors in the US are now favouring a more discreet type of page ornamentation, more likely to be accepted for competitive entries at the lower and middle levels. A number of the fully bordered sheets are shown in *Illustration 8.2*. In *Illustration 8.3* is a purpose-made discreet type of sheet design of a subdued pictorial character, and the method by which it is produced. The upper part shows the motif struck lightly from the handstamp, the lower has the motif completed by hand in ink.

In the case of the traditional stamp collection, the differences between the competitive and the non-competitive sheets relate mainly to the quality of the material and its layout. In thematics, however, there is a very wide range of material which a non-competitive collector may use, but which, being of a collateral nature, is almost inadmissible in a competitive entry. Examples of competitive sheets and of those with a substantial amount of collateral material are shown in this chapter. Collectors interested in competitions should read these notes in conjunction with the material given in the three chapters which follow.

Here is a new point. It concerns the buying of material—i.e. stamps, covers, FDCs, maximum cards, etc. The method, suggested in Chapter 7, of setting up special storepoints for material and information, can be used to secure even more benefits than have been outlined so far. These are described in the section of this chapter under the heading 'The buying focus', on page 116.

If the author were to offer a perpetual contribution to thematic/topical/subject collecting, it would be: 'Stamps and information are the left and right hands of the thematic collector.'

This chapter therefore devotes considerable space to the question of locating thematic information. The seasoned stamp collector will already be aware of most of the problems of finding the stamps. It also includes examples of good and indifferent thematic practice with regard to cancellations, maximum cards and special sheets. In order to save space, the examples have been disassociated from the sheets on which they are normally mounted.

Getting the right stamps into the right order

'With the help of a good check list and a couple of catalogues you should have no problem.' This easy assumption is true only in a very general sense and unfortunately it is of limited value to the collector as an individual. Check lists are usually arranged according to the system which the authors consider the best or which they prefer. Some, in fact, appear to be no more than a collection of information and illustrations on random aspects of the subject. Many contain extremely useful lists of several thousands of stamps which cover the whole range of the topical/subject.

However, the possibility is remote that any collector will wish to arrange his collection on a 'line-by-line basis' like that in the check list. But it should be made clear that it is not the check lists which are at fault, but the lack of a method of using them which is responsible for the defect. There is a further point which needs an answer here. What precisely does a collector do when he finds that a check list has not so far been published on his pet theme/subject/topical? Or has been printed in a language of which he is completely ignorant?

The vital step of finding out which stamps etc. are needed for a particular section of a collection often presents a problem. The particular need is for a method of connecting a very basic and general concept of a part of the collection (as it is envisaged) with a simple list from which stamps can be ordered. So they are compelled to buy materials in a 'worse-than-semi-random' order in the hope that it can 'all be sorted out in due course' and made to fit the story of the theme. That is, of course, if it is even suitable for it. This lack of a suitable method wastes time, money and patience, all of which can be very frustrating. Why let that happen to you? If it does, then you will certainly lose much of your fun and pleasure.

Let's start by expanding the heading of this section to make it apply to you, the reader. Try 'Making a list of the right stamps in the right order to fit your ideas of the collection'. Here is the quickest way (in the long run) to find out which stamps, cancellations, etc. are needed for each section of the collection. There are two stages in this process: the first has two steps in it; the second needs three. The routines for each are stated in simple terms but it is the order of these steps which is so important.

The starting point is the list of the parts in your collection as described in Chapter 7. This list should be as complete as possible, bearing in mind the broadest angles you can envisage for the expansion of the collection. Be generous and build in plenty of allowances for growth and so avoid the annoyance and practical difficulties of having to revise the layout of the collection later on. As a field for inspiration as to how the collection can grow, the reader will find that the Appendix to this book contains the complete breakdowns for four collections. Make a point of comparing these with the breakdown of your own collection, looking for ways that the collection can be usefully expanded. In each case there are comments to give some indication of the collector's personal background, and this will be a useful pointer as to which of the three colllections is the nearest to your own. Do you like exploring the historical aspects of a subject? If so, then the first example, 'The Life and Works of William Shakespeare', may be worth your while for study. In this example, both the 'one-minute' simple list made long before the start of collecting and the current picture of the extensive collection are given. Notice that, as the result of using an historical approach, a very different picture of the make-up of the collection has appeared.

The second collection, 'Bird Life', is typical of an arrangement of a scientific/geographical subject. Note that this subject, and many others like it, can be very satisfactorily set up on the simple basis of that shown in the list in Chapter 7. The long list in the Appendix for this subject is certainly the pride and joy of one particular collector, but it should be in no way regarded as a target. Its function for you is to provide a good hunting ground for ideas about your own collection. The third collection shows the make-up of a simple classified subject 'Textiles', where neither the historical nor the scientific approaches are involved. If the way in which this collection grows appeals to you more than in the other two, then try to get as many 'inspirations' as possible from this collector's list. The fourth collection came into existence from a purely personal liking for the work of a stamp designer, Miss Jennifer Toombes. It adds emphasis to the fact that the subject selected should essentially be one for which there is a strong, clear, personal preference.

Note a useful idea here. The lists in the Appendix illustrate the logical growth order, but it is known that in at least two of them the collector began the assembly of a collection at a point where the 'favourite and most liked material' could be handled. Thus the textile collection began with a spree into the embroidery section, but the collector soon realised where the story really began and added the many other aspects over the course of several years. So do not worry in the slightest if, just at the moment, you have little positive interest in the point where your own story begins. When you think that the list is complete and to your satisfaction make a point of checking that it is in good logical order from the thematic angle and that it starts off with the introduction. Now for the details of this two-stage routine.

STAGE 1, STEP 1

Look down your list and select the facet about which you already know the most. If this happens to be your favourite, as it probably will, then so much the better. (See A on *Illustration 8.4*.) If this is at a point some way down the list do not worry about it, nor try to change your ideas, providing the check of the logical order mentioned earlier was made. It is far better to make a thumping good start at an intermediate point than a thoroughly indifferent one at a supposed beginning. Later on, that poor opening will be very off-putting. Of course, if logicality is the keynote of your life, then you may be compelled to go in right at the start. If so, then experience has clearly shown that the introduction is best tackled at quite a late stage in the process of collection building. The story which the collection must spell out starts with the first part after the introduction. So if 'order, method and more order' suits your bill the best, that is where you collection building must start.

STAGE 1, STEP 2

Now make a précis of all the information you can find on that selected part. (See B of the *Illustration 8.4.*) Extract all the important angles, dates if any, facts and other data you can locate. Concentrate on the facet which you have selected and try not to be side-tracked by the excitements of other highways and byways. Aim to get this précis into an order you understand and feel that it's your way of arranging the bits of information. This completes Stage 1.

STAGE 2, STEP 1

Now turn this précis into a short story, your style (C of *Illustration 8.5*). Tell this in the way you envisage telling it to a friend looking at the collection later on. Even if it requires several trials, get this story right from start to finish. Use the technique of 'first this and then that' in repetition to ensure that you build plenty of continuity into the story, because this is precisely what will hold the stamp version of the story together. At this stage do not worry whether you will ultimately be able to find stamps etc. to illustrate each angle of the story as it develops: that's a matter easily looked after at a later stage.

STAGE 2, STEP 2

In this step (D in the *Illustration 8.5*) it is necessary to isolate all the salient points in your little story and then list them in the order in which they occur. Be on the generous side. Why? Because the success of the job of matching stamps against the salient points requires quite a lot of flexibility and freedom. One forward point is to be sure to keep this list handy during the collecting as it will form an invaluable guide to what is or is not in the collection.

STAGE 2, STEP 3

This produces the basic list of stamps, covers etc. which will be required for the selected part of the collection. With the list of salient points in one hand and a check list plus catalogues in the other, pick out the best stamps to illustrate each point in turn. The author suggests that stamps which are somewhat more expensive than can usually be afforded should be included in the list but those far beyond your means should be left out. Here are two points of note. First, enter the catalogue numbers of all stamps relative to each of the salient points on your list. Knowledge of alternatives may well be invaluable at the sheet layout stage, when those tricky questions of balance and so on are likely to crop up. Next, do not be discouraged if at the moment no more than 30 per cent of the salient points can be illustrated by stamps. The shortfall can be met in two ways: (a) new issues and discoveries; and (b) the use of simple linkages in the writing-up. This latter function is frequently most effective when split between the foot of one sheet and the heading of the next.

What next? Why not take advantage of your freedom as a collector and go ahead exactly as you please? You have the choice of finishing off that single section of the collection on the basis of the list now compiled or gathering further expertise by tackling another section of your collection. Most starter collectors will plump for the former course and then they will have the advantage of seeing what the result of their collection building looks like. And that's good for the enthusiasm too. But there are some merits in the second line of action. Going through the routines of Stage 1 and Stage 2 again will add lots to your ability to sort out stamps against the pattern of the story of the collection. In fact this is the main job of the thematic collector and therefore the chief area in which profits of time and money can be taken. Also it will allow you further opportunities to harmonise one section of the collection with the next. It may be that you feel that you have the focus all set to tackle the very first part of the collection (excluding the introduction of course). It is in fact a good idea to get the early parts of the collection together as soon as possible because this will give you a sizeable amount of the story against which to check the logical order. Now you can put together all these short stories which were produced in Step 1 of Stage 2 and see how they run as a narrative. Here's a good idea. Why not try them out on a collector friend over the completed sheets? Do try to watch the reactions to give you clues as to how good or how poor your collecting efforts have been so far. A little friendly daylight may show you quite a lot.

Handling out-of-the way subjects

A considerable amount of information has now been given on a method of finding out which stamps etc. are needed for specific parts of the collection and making use of a check list as the primary guide. This applies to the 126 subjects shown in the short list in the Appendix. Many of the subjects/topicals/themes not covered by this list are very attractive and unusual. The story which the collection tells about an unusual topic is nearly always a new one and seems to bring with it unlimited pleasure. But the point arises as to how to overcome the absence of a check list as such. Of course, if you choose an out-of-the way subject with its added pleasures and interests, you must expect to encounter just a few more difficulties in getting it successfully off the ground.

Generally, these special subjects can be related to an originating subject of a broader type. The derivative subjects are seen in the following eight forms:

1	classified	2	geographical
3	historical	4	personal
5	political	6	scientific
7	sociological	8	technical

Think about your special subject and try to envisage in which of the eight ways it would be presented in the collection. The easiest way to do this is by eliminating those ways of showing the subject which you are sure that you can neither use nor enjoy. Here is a random example. The subject 'A Tour through Europe', at first sight, suggests that a geographical type of presentation would fill the bill. But if the tour is to see some of the famous paintings, then the geographical angle is only a second runner.

The exercise of eliminating the 'impossible ways of showing' gives the following:

1	classified	2	geographical
3	historical X	4	personal X
5	political X	6	scientific X
7	sociological X	8	technical X

Eliminating the X entries leaves two types (1) classified and (2) geographical. In the classified way of showing the nearest general subject is art. The requirement is therefore to secure a combination of art and geography, with the former markedly predominating. In the short list of subjects (Appendix) locate two subjects which can be shown, the first in the art series and the second the geographical area. The checklists of the two subjects so chosen can then be used to guide you to the stamps, covers etc. which will fit reasonably well into your special need. This is much a matter of finding the clues and getting the inspirations and what better recipe could there be for a session of unlimited exploration, excitement and pleasure?

The buying focus
The buying focus which a collector possesses can have a very marked effect on both the quality and the composition of the resulting collection which he produces. This is not connected with whether he spends a lot of money or a little on the purchase of material nor with any indulgence in bargain snatching by buying first and thinking afterwards.

In connection with the buying focus, the reader is offered the following thoughts. In thematics, is the wisest buying programme strictly related to the immediate progress pattern of collecting? In other words, is it good policy to start buying for only the commencement or early parts of the collection and to ignore the requirements of the middle and later parts? Before answering these questions the author would mention one type of expenditure which he considers justified in all circumstances. Occasional outbursts of spending enthusiasm are an excellent tonic and all collectors are thoroughly entitled to enjoy this sort of pick-me-up now and then.

First, a buying focus which automatically produces the answers to the two questions must be as practical as possible. When considering the buying objectives both time and money need to be taken into account.

As regards money, it will be recalled that thematic material (for a particular subject) can be distinguished as: (a) strongly connected with the subject; (b) connected in a secondary way; and (c) exhibiting only a weak connection. Items which fall into (a) are capable of producing the greatest amount of thematic wealth whilst those at the other end of the scale in (c) can contribute little or nothing to the real value of the collection. It follows therefore that, on a steadily rising market, the maximum possible expenditure on material in (a), whether for immediate use or in the future, must be one of the main planks in the best buying plan. This is so because over the period when the collection is being built, money will be saved and the pro-rata expenditure for material in this category produces the greatest amount of thematic wealth. Conversely, purchasing material in (c) represents the worst buy.

To operate a buying programme successfully, which takes account of both the cash and the thematic wealth angles, means that the collector must have the ability to recognise on sight the correct degree of relevance of each particular item as it comes to light. Nothing but experience can produce this sort of capability, but it is not always essential that getting it should cost money. Take the opportunity, on as many occasions as possible, to make the assessment of relevancy and thematic worth whether a buy is in mind or not. Never buy before making these two assessments of course. As to whether you do so afterwards is quite another matter.

The key point is that this ability to recognise the degree of relevancy (of a stamp, cover etc.) should be used to expand the range and extent of buying and not as a restriction on it. Items which come into the good buy (a) should therefore be taken as a matter of principle even if they fall just outside the present concept of the collection. Next, items in the 'worst buy' (c) should be refused. The money saved is far better spent on items in (a).

As regards the time aspect of the buying focus, the author has always been interested in the phenomenon of the unexpected appearance of certain types of material on the market and the (apparent) disappearance for ever thereafter. This is perhaps a hangover from the days of conservative stamp collecting. In thematics, the need for specific items at any one point in time is spread over a number of parts of the collection and compared with stamp collecting the prospects for successful purchasing are accordingly improved. Why not take advantage of this?

The author suggests that the buying focus for the thematic collector should be:

1   Buy forcefully all items strongly related to the theme, subject or topical, but remember that if they are of a collateral nature they cannot be included in a competitive entry.

2   Avoid buying any items in (c) however infrequently seen on the market.

3   Exercise your options about items in (b) where the connection with the subject is shown only secondarily. Take them on a hunch that research will increase their status; that's one way to fun. Perhaps a better plan is to buy these items according to your estimate of their thematic potential and put them into the stockbook where a useful eye can be kept on them. They have cost you cash and may have more thematic value in the long run than you suppose right now.

Now for the last point in the buying focus for the thematic collector. Certain 'operational' reasons have been suggested for setting up a storepoint with the title 'Waiting Information' and this can provide an excellent holding place for the safekeeping of all the forward buys. These items may well represent a lot of money and time. They are thematic wealth and therefore have an appropriate potential for pleasure and satisfaction. The buying focus suggested in this section of the chapter can therefore be a means of buying wisely now for the pleasures of today as well as those of tomorrow. Or 'The best buys produce the greatest amount of fun, pleasure and satisfaction.'

Sources of supply of material

The two books referred to in the earlier part of this chapter as well as those in the Bibliography contain a considerable amount of general information about the many sources of supplies for the stamp collector. But the real question is 'Where does the topical/thematic/subject collector stand in this important part of collection building? Further, are there any useful buying points to bear in mind?

Accepting that all the information given elsewhere on this subject applies to thematic collectors generally, it is essential to have the following points in mind:

1 The supply prospects are very much better regarding the popular subjects such as space, art, the United Nations and the Americas, than for those which are somewhat unusual—banking or education, for instance.

2 Currently, quite a large number of dealers will welcome wants lists for a certain range of topicals. So look for their notices in the first instance, rather than write to a general stamp dealer 'out of the blue'. Your chances of drawing a blank with the latter are many times greater than with the former.

3 Providing that complete sets and not individual stamps are asked for, many of the dealers cater for about 60 subjects. This type of service is far more easily found in America than in Great Britain.

4 Dealers are not magicians! Despite this, many collectors will buy sets of stamps from their local dealer quite happily. When he wants an unused single which occurs well up in an expensive set he hesitates about asking for it in the home town. So he notes this want and is reluctant to buy the whole set. Soon three or four more of similar status are added to the list and the total need becomes a matter of urgency. In semi-desperation the whole list is sent to a dealer 'who perhaps might like to supply these odd stamps'. In essence you are asking that dealer to break a range (what on earth can he do with the rest of that broken set?) for your enjoyment. How much are you prepared to compensate the dealer for the stamps which you do not want and he cannot sell? Most collectors reply: 'Nothing at all; that's his business.' The wisest thing, of course, is not to send such a request to any dealer, even if you know him personally. You could make a friendly call, just in the hope that there is a spare in the stockbooks, but the author would hesitate before doing even this.

There is no simple, easy way of solving the difficulty of getting the one or two values in a long set without buying the whole issue. But there are a number of ways to find a solution in most cases. Exploit each and every one rather than abandon the hope of ever getting these rather troublesome items. Here are a few ways:

1   If the sheet is not for competitive use, try to find a very fine used copy and use this, even if it means changing all the rest of the items on the sheet which are unused.

2   Make a thorough search for another stamp which will produce the same effect in the collection. This will take time and effort to comb through the catalogues and articles. Sometimes this search will bring to light a better qualified item than the one which is proving so difficult to get. This is the ideal solution.

3   Dealers are not the only source of supply. The circulating packets (in America these are known as circulating lists) of the specialist societies in the thematic area of collecting are sometimes very helpful. Often however, nearly all the collectors of the particular topical/subject are also in urgent need of precisely the same stamp for exactly the same reasons. Solving the problem this way is rather a matter of luck, of course, but then we all enjoy a fair slice of this now and then, so make a point of trying yours when in this kind of difficulty.

4   Sometimes the stamp you need so badly and cannot buy easily in unused condition will be offered to you on a cover along with a number of others. To take it off may well considerably reduce its value. *Illustration 8.6* will show you how to 'disguise' this one stamp so that it can be shown as a single without loss in value. In this example, the Bahamas 5s stamp was needed for the theme of modern transport, but the purchase of the whole set was considered to be quite unjustifiable.

5   If the stamp which is so badly needed proves to be one of the key items in the story the collection is to tell, think over the investment aspect of the set in which it appears. If this has bright prospects, why not buy the whole set, take out the single for your collection and store the balance in a stockbook with a space for the return of that elusive value?

Visual appreciation

Many of the pleasures of collecting spring from the sight of sheets from a collection some of which may be complete, others only partially so. Illustrations are impact-producing devices and it may well be that readers will not only benefit from but also enjoy looking at reproductions of some sheets and other items. The following notes refer to a selection made with an Anglo-American idea in mind and indicate the area in which each may be used.

1   *Colour illustration 6* shows a group of fully pictorial sheets as used in the United States of America for topical collections. Those for transport, animals, railways on stamps and Christmas are reproduced as from collections. This type of sheet is very attractive. The Christmas page, with the large group of stamps and the bars of festive music is especially so. They do, however carry some demerits which have been noted already. The collector is strongly advised not to use this type of sheet in any competitive entry. In a non-competitive collection, however, the matter is quite different. If you like them, use them.

2   By way of a contrast, *Illustration 8.2* is of four fully bordered sheets of a non-pictorial type. Border no. 1 incorporates a crossover device in three thin lines and the general effect of this type is seen at the top of the montage. Border no. 2 consists of a single thin line, no. 3 a single thick line whilst no. 4 combines the thin and thick lines. Compared with the fully pictorial type of sheet, these are more discrete and far less likely to distract attention from the vital components, the stamps and covers. The 'all-round border' tends to restrict the amount of space available and to increase the possibility of overcrowding. Large items such as covers which cut into the border tend to spoil the regularity and so adversely affect general impressions. Used with care, they help to make attractive entries where only a small number of sheets are to be shown. Safety decides against their use in the more important competitions.

3   A purpose-made pictorial sheet for use in a collection of 'The Fire Service in Philately' is shown in *Colour illustration 7*. It has the merit of individuality. But the long ladder, placed at a slope with the longer rungs at the bottom, makes it difficult to

produce a nicely balanced sheet. Matters are eased somewhat if the stamps have a long vertical format and the order is not important. The example given shows the squeezed effect which results when the shape does not entirely favour the collector.

4   The Copernicus sheet as shown in *Colour illustration 8* has the merit of individuality and at the same time allows the stamps to be fully objective. There is no restriction on the space available for mounting the stamps but the faint blue background requires blue lettering in the writing-up. This has the minor defect that it does not attract attention as well as the normal black ink. In the non-competitive areas of collecting this is not important. An exhibit of a large number of this type of sheet, however, would have an all-over grey effect, which adversely affects general impression.

5   *Colour illustration 9* shows the British Honduras miniature sheet, from the tree and humanity collection, and has the merit of providing more information about each type of tree than is shown on the stamps. Each quarter of the sheet shows the tree, the leaves, flowers and fruit as well as the sort of wood which can be obtained from it. It is therefore a thematic maximum.

9 Local Society/Chapter and Federation Competitions

This chapter title is used as a matter of convenience and is only loosely indicative of its type and range of material. It is the best the author can devise to cover organised collecting in both Great Britain and America. In the United States of America the organisation of the small groups of collectors is met by two types, either town local societies or chapters of a larger body. These chapters are branch groups of the parent organisation. The two major bodies so concerned are the American Philatelic Society, with some 600 chapters catering for all types of collectors, and the American Topical Association, with chapters for the topicals. It is therefore reasonable to regard the local societies of Great Britain and the chapters of America as roughly equivalent types of organisation from the competitive aspect. The ATA chapters have competitions within themselves, as part of a larger exhibition but using the ATA rules and judges. The only ATA-sponsored exhibition is TOPEX and this is therefore equivalent to a national event.

There are two parts to this chapter. The first covers the local society/chapter type of event and the second the larger and more advanced competitions staged at federation exhibitions.

The local society/chapter type of competition
These are generally organised by non-national groups of collectors who usually are not strongly competitively minded. Although there are only a few entries the important factor is that the maximum number of sheets which can be entered for these events is relatively small and in the range of 8 to 12 per entry. The society usually has a programme which contains both collecting and social components, with about 100 or so members on the books, of whom less than half may attend any

one meeting. The number of competition entries for all classes is usually in the vicinity of a dozen. There are several types of organisation from which a small number of competitive entries result but these are of a rather specialised type. This differs from that of a local society/chapter very considerably and is not covered here. Thus the specialist society entries are of an even, high standard closely related to the organisation's interest and not to thematics in general. There are also a number of very large world-wide organisations and competitive events are not therefore very feasible. Also in this category are the large, closely knit societies who stage competitions favoured by the more advanced collectors in the group. These also tend to produce specialised entries, which are outside the scope of this book.

The reader may have noticed that care has been taken to avoid the suggestion that these small, friendly competitions should be considered as comprising the lowest level in the competitive world. Although this is nearly always true, the attachment of a label of this sort may well be considered as faintly suggestive of class distinction and the author wishes avoiding such implication. Now for the competitions and their requirements.

The first essential, of course, is to look at the background of these local society/chapter competitions as distinct from the ATA chapter events. Although many of these are staged annually, not all cater for topical/thematic collectors by providing a set of rules and judging criteria separately from those for stamps and postal history. In those cases where one set of rules applies to all classes of entry, the judging criteria must be of a general character and possess some degree of flexibility. For the thematic entrant, they are usually quite easily met and present no difficulty. Nevertheless, the entry should be prepared with the criteria laid down well in mind. When the judging requirements are more precise, and specific criteria set out for thematic entries, these can vary widely between one society and another. No good purpose would therefore be served by including sample rules. Before commencing the preparation of their entry, intending competitors should make a point of securing a copy of the rules relative to the competition in mind. And make good use of them too! The ATA chapters, of course, provide the rules and judging criteria for the competitions and the members should therefore be excellently briefed as to what is required.

The fact that the number of sheets which can be entered in these competitions is limited to 8–12 produces three effects which are important for the thematic/subject/topical collector. These are:

1 It is a prime requirement that thematic-type entries should tell a story or show a series of connected steps in the subject/topical group of sheets. It is therefore essential that the sheets should be specially selected with this in mind. To extract them from odd points in the collection because they are the most attractive can only produce a picture which is somewhat disconnected and not easy to understand. The judges will find this off-putting with an adverse effect on the marking. To guard against this eventuality, the selection should preferably be drawn from one part of the collection. If this is of a general character, rather than of an unusual or complicated nature, so much the better.

2 The second important point is connected to the first. Within the limits of the small number of sheets which can be submitted, it is difficult to demonstrate the logical development of a theme or the progressive pattern of the topical/subject. In this connection, the latter two types of entry are somewhat easier to handle than the theme. Much can be done, however, by preparing a special set of sheets for the entry, with links between them in the writing-up.

3 The third point is that, with the restricted number of sheets on which to accommodate the whole of the entry, it is uneconomic to allow more than half of the first for the introduction. The introduction is an important item and the wise competitor will therefore have no hesitation in preparing one which fits each type of competition entry in which he is involved. *Colour illustrations 10* and *11* show how the full-page introduction to a non-competitive collection had to be redesigned for a local competition.

In a somewhat different connection, it is of note that, invariably, the judges are provided with a copy of the rules and are expected to work from them when assessing the merit of the entries. On the other hand, for one reason or another, the competitors do not or seem not to take them into account. Good local society judges know that one of the important functions of these competitions is to encourage the competitors and to avoid too much discouragement. They therefore have to make a shrewd balance between the need to encourage the competitors on the one hand and evalue the true thematic worth on the other. Such allowances have to be made as are thought appropriate for each occasion and some competitors, especially those at the lower end of the scale of marks, fail to appreciate the necessity for the judges to do so. The answer, of course, is for these complainants to ensure that they are at the top and not at the bottom.

The general impression of an entry can be important, and in some competitions as high as 25 per cent of the total marks may be awarded for this. Experience shows that many competitors fail to notice defects in their entries which the judges invariably detect and take into account on the adverse side when considering 'general impression'. It is wise, therefore, to make a special test of the impression of the entry before it is completed, preferably in the drafting stage. When viewed from a central point about 5 or 6 feet away (2 metres), the sheets should be seen to run in a harmonious pattern with a little allowance for the first or introductory sheet. Any sheet which compels undue attention at this distance will detract from the value of the entry by denying the rest of the sheets their due share of notice. This over effectiveness can be produced in a number of ways. The first, shown at A in *Illustration 9.1,* arises from an excess of material on the page. Overcrowding is usually penalised far more than the pronounced shortage of material, as shown in B, which produces the large white area that invariably commands undue attention. The third, C, shows the damaging effect on presentation and general impression caused by a large, brightly coloured cover which must of necessity be placed at an angle on the sheet.

The general impression test is not the only one used to determine the merit of an entry. Nearly always it is followed by a detailed examination which assesses the merit of each sheet against the several judging criteria. Some allowance has to be made, of course, for the first or introductory sheet. This is the most important single sheet in the entry. It should give a brief clear introduction to the entry, then a statement of the intent and scope of the exhibit and also a description of the arrangement over the sheets. It goes without saying that the title or introductory sheet must give an entirely accurate picture of those which follow it. Flowery, over-ornamental or woolly terminology is best avoided. Amusing title pages do not usually result in the same amount of credit as one which is short, precise, effective and complete.

Enthusiasm for competitive events is excellent and most commendable. Full of eagerness to put up a good entry which will convince the judges that it has outstanding merit, there is a natural tendency for the collector to try to get the maximum amount of material on to the small number of sheets permitted. In this sort of competition the temptation to produce overcrowding is very great. The practical point, however, is this: just what constitutes overcrowding? This is perhaps more important than knowing what causes it. In general, a greater amount of material per sheet may be acceptable at the society/chapter level, than at federation or national levels. In the other direction, a sheet which would be considered as quite satisfactory (in this respect) at a national competition could well be scored as lacking in interest and needing more material at the local/chapter event. *Illustrations 9.2* and *9.3* show two such sheets.

Federation events
The term 'federation' or 'association' as such may apply to a wide variety of organisations. Thus it can comprise a few constituent societies meeting in a restricted part of the country, or cover a national area such as is served by the British Philatelic Federation—or an even more widespread one, such as that from which the American Topical Association draws its membership. The one with the widest possible interest is the Fédération Internationale de Philatélie which has nearly 60 member countries. It should be noted that the type of organisation referred to here as a federation chapter resembles the first of those mentioned above and results from the

collective activities of a small compact group of local societies. These federations, like the local societies, make up their membership from a common geographical and social/collector type of identity.

Because federation events are much in the nature of an extension of those run by local societies or chapters, a considerable amount of the information given in the earlier part of this chapter also applies to them. The entries in these federation competitions are usually drawn from the more successful of those at the society level but from a very much wider area. The overall standard is therefore higher and more even, from the thematic merit point of view, than is found at the lower level. Because of this, it may well work out that the winner in the federation competition possesses only slightly more merit than many of the other entries. The value of these competitions is not so much in the relative overall grading but in the assessments made by the judges of individual entries against the several judging criteria.

Usually, judges are drawn from an adjacent and similar organisation being of good philatelic/thematic standing, and are selected as being competent for the task. As a result, the entries, all of which did very well in their local society/chapter event, are now subject to judging of a higher calibre and with a more critical eye than before. The judges also have more regard for the substance and the intention of the rules and criteria which govern the competition and minor departures from them are not so easily overlooked as in the local society events. Very frequently, one or more of the judges may have served on the jury of a national exhibition and his expressions of opinion about the merit of the entries will tend to be pointed towards the higher level rather than the lower. To some extent, therefore, the federation type of competition can be considered as a preparatory step to those of the national exhibitions. But it must be noted that the nationals not only require many more sheets to be submitted, and also a higher standard of thematic merit, but certain judging criteria not in evidence at the federation level are regarded as important.

Before considering the detailed requirements of these federation competitions there are two general points which deserve thought. First, the maximum number of sheets

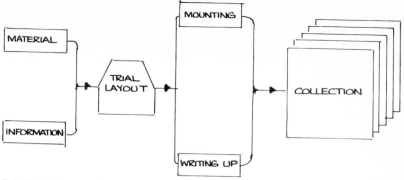

7.2 The basic route into the collection

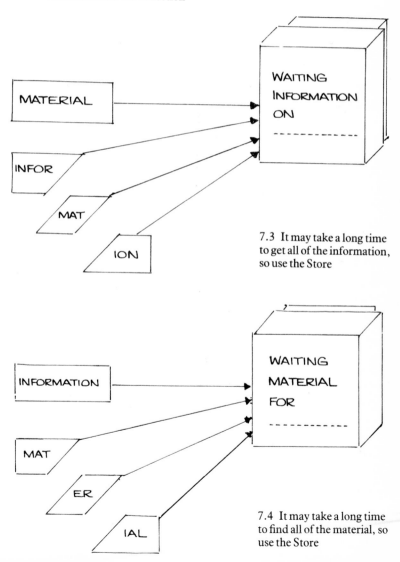

7.3 It may take a long time to get all of the information, so use the Store

7.4 It may take a long time to find all of the material, so use the Store

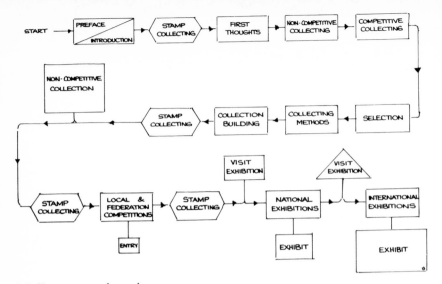

8.1 Your route to thematics

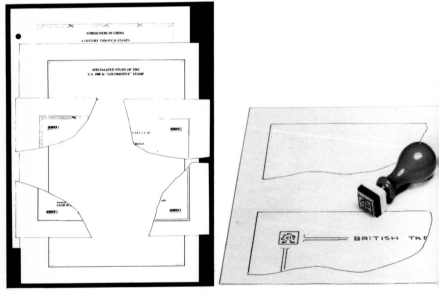

8.2 The subdued all-round borders

8.3 Method of producing a discreet personal motif

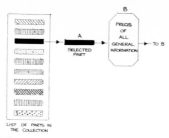

LIST OF PARTS IN
THE COLLECTION

8.4 The two stage routine; letters A–B

8.5 The two stage routine; letters C–E

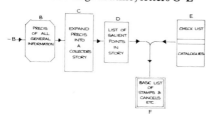

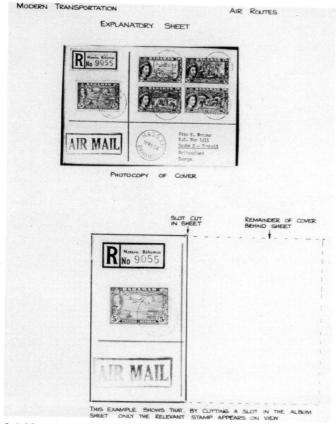

MODERN TRANSPORTATION   AIR ROUTES

EXPLANATORY   SHEET

PHOTOCOPY   OF   COVER

SLOT CUT
IN SHEET

REMAINDER OF COVER
BEHIND SHEET

THIS EXAMPLE SHOWS THAT, BY CUTTING A SLOT IN THE ALBUM
SHEET   ONLY THE RELEVANT STAMP APPEARS ON VIEW

8.6 Now to show a single stamp on a cover separated from
a number of others

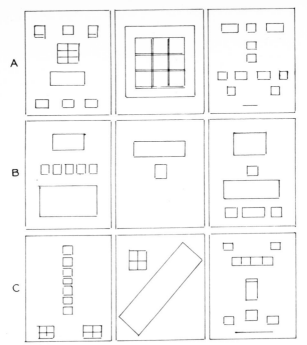

9.1 What to avoid with page layouts. *Row A, centre sheet:* excess of material. *Row B, centre sheet:* excess white space detracts. *Row C, centre sheet:* cover at an angle diverts attention

9.2 A sheet satisfactory for a national exhibition but not for a local competition

9.3 Another sheet that would be satisfactory for a national competition

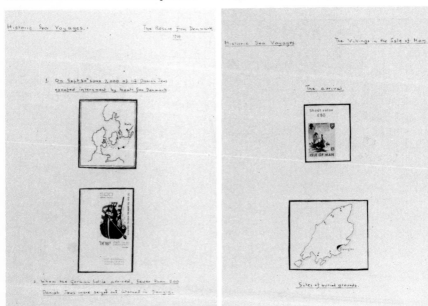

<u>EARNEST SHACKLETON</u>

<u>BRITISH ANTARCTIC EXPEDITION   1907-09</u>

<u>BRITISH IMPERIAL TRANS-ANTARCTIC EXPEDITION   1914-16</u>

<u>SHACKLETON-ROWETT ANTARCTIC EXPEDITION   1921-22</u>

Shackleton was born in Ireland in 1874. As a young boy he quickly tired of school and left to go
to sea. While still in his early twenties he found his challenge at the unattained South Pole.

Def Issue   Feb 73

In 1902 Shackleton was a member of Robert F. Scott's *Discovery* Expedition. On 30th December
1902, Scott, Shackleton, and Dr Edward Wilson reached farther south than anyone before them but
they had to return due to bad weather.

Def Issue   Jul 67

Explorers series booklet   Aug 1969

Def Issue   Feb 54

9.4 Balance of sheet disturbed by booklet

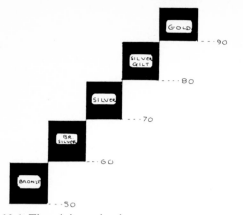

10.1 The minimum levels for the award of medals

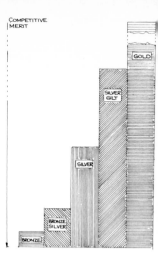

10.2 The amount of competitive merit

SEVENTEENTH CENTURY -- THE THERMOMETER; THOUGHTS ON ATMOSPHERIC PRESSURE

The few advances in meteorology made in the two-thirds of a century between da Vinci's death and the appearance of Galileo were often hampered by insistence in following without question the word of Aristotle.

Galileo

Early experiments with the air thermoscope were made by Galileo in the 1590's. This device indicated changes in temperature by changes in the water level in a vertical tube. Such a device could not be called a thermometer until it was equipped with some kind of a scale.

Galileo had made an air thermometer by 1613, but writings indicate Santorio had added a scale prior to 1612. However it is to Galileo that the invention of the thermometer is accorded.

Two Descartes printings:

The French philosopher Rene Descartes had a great influence on the science of the 17th Century. His <u>Discourse on Method</u> contains the bases that were to lead to development of the calculus.

As did so many of the scientific inquirers of the day, Descartes delved into many fields. In response to a student's query, he wrote (1631) that the mercury in a vertical tube closed at its upper end does not fall out because of a "subtle matter that pervades all space." The mercury is supported to a height governed by the air "from that point to above the clouds."

Issued 9 June 1937; correct book title.

Issued 10 June 1937; incorrect book title.

10.3 Example of an overwritten sheet

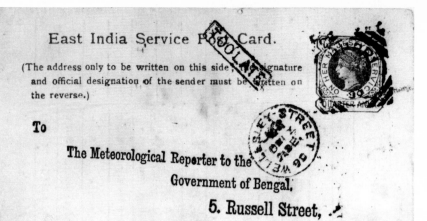

East India Service Post Card.

(The address only to be written on this side, the signature
and official designation of the sender must be written on
the reverse.)

To

The Meteorological Reporter to the
Government of Bengal,
5. Russell Street,
CALCUTTA.

10.4 Use of a postcard and collateral material

M. R. O. No. 6.
FORM G.
METEOROLOGICAL OBSERVATION
taken at _Dhubr_ (Station).
Date _mon_ day, the 22nd of _Sep_ 1890

Barometer	8 A. M.	29·820
Attached Thermometer	8 A. M.	79·0
Dry bulb "	8 A. M.	77·9
Wet bulb "	8 A. M.	75·8
Max. Ther. in shade reading of previous day taken at 8 A. M.		81·0
Min. Ther. (Read at 8 A. M.)		76·5
Wind Direction	8 A. M.	NE
Anemometer Miles since 8 A. M. of preceding day.		239·4
Rain since 8 A.M. previous day.		0·05
Cloud proportion	8 A. M.	10
Weather Symbol	8 A. M.	4
Weather of preceding 24 hours.		dark floeing weather
Signature.		allen
Designation.		observer

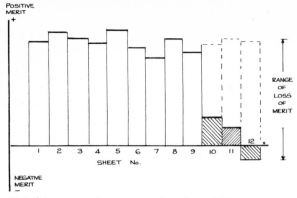

10.5 Diagrammatic representation of an exhibit which loses merit because of poor quality of material at the end

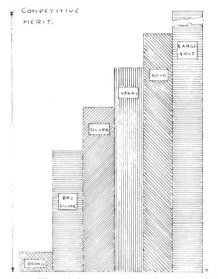

11.1 The minimum requirements for medals

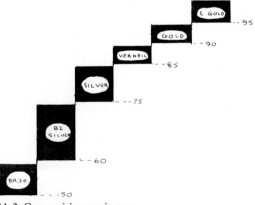

11.2 Competitive merit steps

permitted in these events may be about the same as those for the society competitions. When this is so, the opportunity should be taken to review the introduction so as to ensure that it makes a good impression on the more discerning type of judge now involved. Any excess of descriptive matter of a general nature in the introduction should be replaced to advantage by the more precise. Further, the space saved can be used to expand the thematic technicalities of the entry.

Presentation is one factor which can make a very considerable contribution to the success of an entry and there is much valuable advice on this in the books already recommended for further reading and guidance. Space here will allow for only two of the more important angles to be covered in this chapter. These are (a) the use of the popular pictorially bordered sheets; and (b) the meaning of the term 'balance', its effect on good presentation and how to overcome the problem of defective balance.

As regards (a) some examples of the pictorial borders are shown in *Colour illustrations* 6 and 7. To many of the collectors in the UK, especially those who have not previously seen this type of album sheet, they may well appear to have more a novelty than a thematic value. The surface of these thin cards is excellent for mounting purposes, the quality of the printing is generally very high. Although they tend to restrict the amount of space available for mounting the stamps and especially covers, and the brightly coloured border distracts attention from the thematic items, they are very attractive when used for a non-competitive collection. As regards their use for competitive purposes, an impression is growing in America that they are becoming less and less in favour even at society levels. As a result, the owners of collections which make extensive use of these pictorial sheets need seriously to consider the need to remount all the material intended for competitive purposes. In Great Britain, where the eye of severity is often so clearly in evidence, the use of these sheets in any competition whatsoever would be a matter of considerable risk.

In the main, collectors are both reasonable and progressive. The author is indebted to a well known American collector for two ideas about pictorial borders. In mind is a border which is much more subdued and discreet and yet allows an expression of the personality of the owner or of the subject of the collection. In essence, the printed pictorially bordered sheet is abandoned completely in favour of a plain, white thin card. This carries a small personal motif at each of the top corners with a thin single black-line border. On those sheets which mark the commencement of each part of the collection a further element of individuality can be introduced. Here the thin black borderline at the top and the left-hand side is replaced by the main and sub-titles. The method of producing the motif is of note. A small inexpensive rubber stamp is used for the design. This is applied to the sheet when only partially inked so that a faint impression results. This impression is then drawn over by hand with full black ink. In this way all the motifs, being small and quite regular, remain unobtrusive and have a subdued attraction as shown by *Illustration 8.3*.

Now for the very practical matter of balance. In thematics, each stamp or group of stamps must illustrate a step in the story of the theme or a component of the topical/subject. It is most desirable that nothing should prevent the nice appreciation of the purpose and function of any item on a sheet of the collection. But stamps, covers, etc., vary very widely in size, colour and density and hence some are very much more attractive to the eye than others. Few sheets contain sets of stamps of a uniform size and colour and many must accommodate six, seven or eight items of unrelated size and colours. The problem of securing an even distribution of their attractiveness can be tackled by considering that each sheet has imaginary central, vertical and horizontal axes. The stamps, covers, etc. are then selected and placed on the sheet so that the size/colour objectiveness above this central horizontal axis is balanced by that below it. Similarly, the objectiveness of the left-hand side of the imaginary vertical axis should balance that on the right. This is fine in theory but in practice, because of the thematic significance of each item, this nice balance is not always easy to secure. In these cases, the best compromise possible must be made. *Illustration 9.4* shows a sheet from a collection on Antarctica where the inclusion of the strongly coloured booklet tends to destroy the balance and to upset the harmony of the whole sheet. There are several solutions to this problem. One way of tackling it is to find, if possible, a stamp about as big and bright as the offending booklet and redesign the whole sheet to secure the best possible balance. Another way is to reposition the items so that the booklet is placed in a central position and thus contributes an equal part of its attractiveness to each half of the sheet. *Colour illustration 12* shows a sheet produced with thought about balance well in mind.

A good balance is relatively easy to obtain if the use of special odd-shaped items such as covers, special sheets or cancellations is avoided, but the inclusion of a limited number of these items in the collection is often highly desirable. Besides adding to the thematic value, they can also very effectively break up an otherwise dull and unattractive run of sheets. In competitive work the judicious placing of such items is invaluable.

There is one further point which is useful to keep in mind. Very often the local/chapter and federation competitions are based on a set of criteria which may be the same or very similar. At the lower level, these are usually dominated by the need for the entry to tell a simple story and to be presented neatly and clearly. The position in the federation event alters. Here the requirements of good presentation, logical approach, philatelic merit and completeness are taken much more into account. Accordingly, entries from the local society competitions which are not strong in these judging criteria may fail to attract an award in the federation event, despite a high placing earlier. The remedy, of course, is to strengthen the entry in the weak aspects before entering it in the next level of competition.

10 National Exhibitions

This chapter relates, in general rather than in detail, to the large national exhibitions held in Great Britain and America. The relationship between exhibitions in the two countries, however, must of necessity be rather loose, especially in respect of the American exhibitions where the competitive aspect of thematic/topical collecting is considerably larger and more complex than in Great Britain. In order to allow the maximum amount of practical detail to be covered, opportunity has been taken to use certain aspects of the two British national exhibitions as examples. That the substance of this chapter corresponds rather more closely to the British than the American competitions is the result of expediency and not of preference.

The conditions and disciplines of national exhibitions tend towards those of the internationals and awards at the former are often considered to be stepping stones to the latter. With this in mind, a number of practical aspects of competitive thematics which may well be of use to exhibitors in both types of event have been spread over this chapter and that on internationals. It is hoped that readers, whichever level of competition they have in mind, will read both chapters, selecting the parts most useful.

Typical of the national exhibitions to which this chapter refers are (a) the British Philatelic Exhibition (BPE); (b) Stampex Exhibition; (c) that sponsored by the American Topical Association (TOPEX); and (d) the Inter-American Philatelic Federation's annual event (EXFILBO). Each issues a prospectus setting out the relative rules and regulations which should be studied by the intending exhibitor. One point to note is that both the British exhibitions are open to all-comers, without a qualifying standard or invitation, while another is that the ATA rules as applied at TOPEX and the chapter events do not admit 'one country' exhibits. It is evident from the names of these four exhibitions that whereas those in (a), (b) and (d) are general philatelic exhibitions with topical/thematic classes, the ATA event at TOPEX is exclusively thematic.

Award of medals and degrees of merit

The relationship between the awards standards and the amount of exhibition merit and thematic expertise is of considerable interest. First, it must be emphasised that each entry is considered on its merits and not in comparison with any other entry. The prospectus which is used as the sample gives the following table of the minimum number of marks to secure an award:

Gold medal	90
Silver-gilt	80
Silver	70
Bronze-silver	60
Bronze	50
Other awards	
Diploma of Merit	40

(None of these apply to junior classes)

Marks are arranged in steps of 10 at each stage and it is desired to focus attention on the medal group from 50 (bronze) to 90 (gold). These groups of 10 marks can be illustrated as a series of rising steps from the bronze to the gold as shown in *Illustration 10.1*. A common framework of judging criteria, with a specified proportion for each element, applies to the whole range of awards. Marks within this framework, up to 100, are given to each entry. In the absence of specific information, it appears that the award of a particular grade of medal is related to two interconnected factors. These are (a) the number of marks; and (b) a broader factor which might be termed the total competitive merit in the eyes of the jury. In other words factor (b) is the sum of all that is good in an entry less that which is not satisfactory. This total thematic competition merit governs both the award made and the number of marks accredited to the entry. It is therefore of prime importance to the exhibitor.

The experiences of many collectors suggest that, although the award steps published are in equal amounts of 10 marks over the whole range from the bronze medal to the gold, the amount of competition merit in each step is not so equally related. An increasing amount of merit appears to be required as the scale rises. *Illustration 10.2* shows the amount of competitive merit per step which experience suggests may well apply. This diagram has no true scale and it cannot be applied directly to the previous one which shows the 5 equal 10 mark steps.

When looking at this illustration, notice that the amount of thematic merit required to get from the silver medal level to the silver-gilt is much more than that needed to pass brom the bronze to the bronze-silver stage. The attainment of the gold medal standard calls for even more added merit. Thus some exhibitors, after early successes at the lower levels, express the thought: 'Whatever I do to improve my entry it never gets a better award.' Quite incorrectly they may be trying to relate their latest series of improvements to those which were so successful at the lower level. What is really needed is an appreciation of the total amount of merit needed to attain the next step up. This is where the significance of the columns shown in *Illustration 10.2* is so important. Experience suggests that it would be wise to appreciate its message before embarking on competitive thematics in either national or international areas.

How much merit can an entry and its owner produce? The total amount of exhibition merit of an entry depends on, first of all, the nature of the topic/theme subject and then on the amount of thematic expertise of the owner. Here are some thoughts about each.

Nature of the subject
Not all subjects (in the general sense) have high award-winning potentials. Subject/topical entries vary widely in this respect and the matter contained in the earlier part of the book gives a fair indication of the suitability of any particular type of subject and its development for competitive use. Theme entries have a rather greater potential for attracting merit, but only if the logical development and choice of material are worthy of an

award. Whether you have a theme, topic or subject in mind, do not suppose that potential winners fall out of the sky with a gold medal tag attached to them. They require a lot of time and thought as well as much detailed work to find the material and to arrange it satisfactorily, and all this before the latest date of submission of the entry.

Ability of the owner
Irrespective of the nature of the exhibit, the owner must make his contribution by way of first identifying in his mind the various components of the subject entry, or the steps in the story of the theme, and then the way they should be assembled clearly to indicate his intentions. Having visualised the items needed, then comes the problem of finding them on sale as well as being able to afford them. Last, and here the practical capability of the owner is put to the test, he must have the ability to present the material on the sheets of the exhibit so that he is given maximum credit in the judging. Good material of the right calibre in capable hands nearly always results in a good win; hence the pleasure and satisfaction of competitive thematics.

The stamp content must predominate
The most important requirement in thematics is that the stamp content predominates. An exception to this, of course, is when an historical exhibit is concerned and used material, covers, etc., are then a necessity. What exactly does this phrase 'must predominate' really mean? Predominance is regulated by two simple factors. The first is the number of stamps in relation to the number of other items—including covers, drawings, miniature and souvenir sheets, maximum cards, cancellations and maps etc. The other factor, fully explained earlier, is the share of objectiveness which the stamps secure in relation to all other items on each page.

The following details of an exhibit of philatelic meteorology give a picture of the desirable ratio of stamps to other items in an award-winning entry.

(a) Number of sheets in the entry—80, set up in 5 frames, each of 16 sheets.

(b) Number of stamps per frame (in frame order)—50 + 29 + 52 + 29 + 36 = 196 in all.

(c) *Average number of stamps per sheet = 2.5 approximately.* (The significance of these figures should not escape the reader.)

(d) Number of covers—1 + 4 + 6 + 6 +7 = 24 (about 5 per frame of 16 sheets).

(e) Number of maximum cards—1.

(f) Number of postcards—7.

(g) Number of meter cancellation—6.

(h) Number of documents—1. On examination, this item was considered to be so well related to the subject that its inclusion was considered well justified.

(i) Number of diagrams, miniature sheets and souvenir sheets—nil.

(j) Ratio of stamps to all other items = $^{196}/_{39}$ (*the stamp component comprised 83 per cent of the total number of items included in the entry*).

The importance of the fact that, in this gold entry, well over 75 per cent of the items on the show were unused stamps cannot be overlooked. Also, that they were reasonably well spread over the sheets—see (b) earlier—contributed a considerable amount to the pleasing general impression of the exhibit. A few of the sheets were considered by the owner to be a little overwritten and one of these is shown in *Illustration 10.3*. In particular the second and final paragraphs could be reduced to advantage by at least two lines of matter.

The reader should note that this presentation, especially the amount of writing-up, achieved success at national level and that further reductions might well be made if the entry is intended for an international.

A further point abstracted from this exhibit emphasises the point that non-philatelic material should not normally be included in the entry. A postcard used in the East India Meteorological Service (shown in *Illustration 10.4*) provided excellent evidence very relative to the subject of the exhibit, but this was reinforced by showing the reverse of the card and clearly indicating that the item and the posts were a vital part of the meteorological service.

Relative importance of judging criteria

In order that the exhibitor shall have a guide as to what the judges will use as their yardstick, most of the exhibition prospectuses include details of the criteria laid down. The example given here has been taken from the publication issued by a national exhibition. Here are the details:

Presentation and general impression		15
Extent and scope of the exhibit		15
Development of the exhibit		25
Originality		15
Philatelic elements		
1 Knowledge	10	
2 Presence of philatelic items including rare stamps and their condition	20	30
		100

It is of note that, although the prospectus for this exhibition very clearly defined both a theme and a subject entry, a common set of judging criteria applies to both types. Intending entrants to internationals, however, should observe that this is not so and details of the separate criteria are given in the next chapter.

The two criteria which contribute just over 50 per cent of the (possible) marks are: development with 25; and philatelic elements with 30. A brief thought is that careful attention to these two criteria will pay dividends; lack of attention may mean the imposition of penalties.

Development of the entry

The way the theme or the subject is seen to unfold over the complete range of the sheets is termed the development. This is considered to be good if:

1 *It consists of a series of positive steps* which link themselves together, from start to finish, to make up the complete story and which do not require undue effort or time on the part of the judges to enable them fully to appreciate the nature of the entry. Each step may require one or more sheets of stamps etc. to

secure a nicely sufficient (and no more) illustration of what it is desired to convey.

2   *The steps in the development are clearly in evidence.* This can be helped by the provision of sub-titles on each page that a new aspect begins and, occasionally, by adding a footnote, of a thematic nature, to lead from the last sheet of one step to the first of the next.

3   *The steps are arranged in a logical order according to the nature of the entry.* These types are described in Chapter 6 and examples are given in the Appendix of collections based on four of them. The following thoughts may also be valuable when considering the development.

When thinking about the layout over the whole of the exhibit, there are two targets on which the eye must be kept. The one paramount requirement is that a progressive and logical development from immediately after the introductory page(s) is secured. The other demands that, in respect of thematic merit, no sheet shall be of a noticeably lower standard than any other, nor shall a sheet make a negative contribution in this respect. For example, a badly overcrowded sheet (a near criminal offence in national and international exhibitions) may very well provide an excellent piece of development, but damage the presentation so badly that it incurs a penalty. The good thematic exhibitor will arrange the material on such sheets so that there is no overcrowding yet at the same time the loss to the development is minimal.

4   *Tail-end loss of merit.* Each sheet or group of sheets which make up the steps of the development should contribute equally well to the total amount of merit. An entry which makes a glorious showing and has an excellent development in the first half but thereafter becomes mediocre and fails to live up to the fine earlier pattern is said to be ill-balanced in this respect. The bright start in no way cancels out the quality/development failure at the tail end. *Illustration 10.5* shows in graph form where the quality of the material and the type peter out increasingly over the last three sheets. These are shown as hatched columns. This kind of entry can occur when the exhibitor is unable to produce the required number of sheets, all clearly of the same quality as in the main part of the entry. Rather than advertise the fact that he is short of material he has

added the three sheets at the end which, although they are on the same subject, do not tie in with the rest. Thus both quality of material and development fall off at the tail of the exhibit, a result which ought to be avoided. This loss of merit has a further unsatisfactory aspect. It is quite reasonable to think that if the exhibitor had taken adequate time and care in the preparation stages, sufficient good material strongly connected to the theme/subject could have been found to convert the last three sheets into a very good finish. This is shown in dotted lines with the negative merit of the last sheet converted to a very creditable positive. Judges are well aware that finding good material for the tail end of an exhibit is much more difficult than for the start and the loss resulting from the use of the three sheets of poor thematic quality is therefore considerable.

Introductory sheet(s)

After deciding, in some detail, satisfactory development of the exhibit, the first individual sheet which requires thought is that of the introduction. If space allows, the introduction proper can nicely be preceded by a title sheet. A good introduction to the exhibit in a national event is equally important as in an international exhibition but the content should be rather less explanatory. The reader will find the types of introduction for a theme exhibit and a subject exhibit are covered at some length in the next chapter on internationals and use therefore should be made of this for entries to national exhibitions.

Philatelic elements

Marks are awarded under two headings: (a) knowledge; and (b) presence of philatelic items including rare stamps in good condition. A maximum of 10 marks are given for the first and 20 for the latter. Clearly with a 30 per cent loading these two items cannot be considered lightly.

Although an allowance of 10 marks for philatelic knowledge is not a very great proportion, there is evidence that doubt exists in many exhibitors' minds as to what really constitutes this kind of knowledge. There is one primary observation which should be noted: that the information given in the catalogue, although without doubt philatelic knowledge, is scarcely markworthy in the national exhibition field. On the other hand, little known or new (exhibitor-discovered) information is invaluable. When such important pieces of information are to be shown, if necessary the catalogue details may be omitted for the sake of clarity. Good presentation can also be helped and overcrowding avoided by such omissions.

Presence of philatelic items

It is very easy to include a considerable quantity of philatelic items in an exhibit; it is even easier to completely spoil the whole of the sheets by so doing. Each item which it is proposed to include must prove without doubt that it is not only relative to the theme/subject/topical but that it adds a material amount of thematic merit to the entry. Thus covers, maximum cards, miniature sheets etc., which can be picked up from almost any dealer or appear widely in sales lists, despite the fact that they are philatelic items, add nothing to an entry for a national exhibition. But covers which are elusive or rare, such as that shown in *Illustration 1.2* concerning the Transit of Venus are unquestionably of considerable value. Put at the correct point in a story of astronomy and mankind, it fills the bill very well. Essays and proofs are good for inclusion if they are not only clearly relative to the subject but also justify inclusion as such. The latter point is important. To do so conveys credit also on the exhibitor that he had the foresight not only to suspect that a suitable proof, essay etc. existed but also to find it. Some subjects lend themselves to the inclusion of philatelic items. An exhibit with the title 'The Progress of Printing' will allow a whole range of proofs, essays, flaws and the like to be properly included.

A document is not a philatelic item and as such never will be. But shown on a stamp, it is fully and creditably represented.

Harmful, improper and undesirable issues

National exhibitions are recognised as being stepping stones to international events. The organisers of the former have, therefore, rather wisely, warned intending exhibitors about these issues and that including them may lead to a penalty. In America, issues which have been black blotted are similarly considered. It is unwise of the owner of a thematic exhibit to shrug his shoulders and forget about the ban on these issues. In fact he is particularly vulnerable because of the freedom he enjoys to range over the issues of any country or period for suitable material. Judges at international events usually exact quite severe penalties for infringements of the FIP regulations about these issues. In national exhibitions, where conditions are a little less stringent and the competition not so strong, the inclusion of one or two items may well not attract much attention. But it is far wiser and safer to avoid the use of any stamp or sheet listed as harmful, improper or undesirable. If its place can be filled with a good example for a regular issue, credit is added to the entry rather than taken off.

National exhibitions are not only for the exhibitor
Besides providing the focal point for exhibitors they also give a lot of pleasure and interest to visitors. Unlike the internationals, where at least three or four days are required to make a reasonable examination of the majority of the entries, the national exhibition calls for far less time and effort to see thoroughly. For a visitor, pleasure and enjoyment come sooner rather than later. The very best plan is to allow plenty of time to see the thematic exhibits and to do so easily, constructively or critically, according to taste. If in so doing you learn something about this subject or that theme, all well and good. But in any case you may well leave the exhibition venue in a satisfied and happy frame of mind.

11 International Exhibitions

The term 'international' is correct for the description of an event open to competitors throughout the world. Without further qualification the use conveys no indication of the size and status of the organisation. But what is more important from the competitors' angle is that the simple use of 'international' in itself conveys no indication of the true worth of the awards scheduled to be made.

This chapter relates to only those very large exhibitions which contain not less that 3,000 frames for a general exhibition or 1,500 frames for a specialised thematic event. They must also conform to a published pattern of regulations (or rules) and be designed to have the interests of the competitors and of the public, as well as those of the organisers, at heart. An event can only be called international when these two very simple, general conditions obtain.

Currently, the only organisation known to meet these very simple requirements is the Fédération Internationale de Philatélie (FIP) and use is made here of the information given in *Bulletin No. 1* of Amphilex '77, which was organised by the Netherlands Federation of Philatelic Societies under the patronage of the FIP. In this connection it should be noted that it is the organising body and not the FIP which sets up the exhibition and conducts the business with the competitors and other exhibitors.

The whole area of international thematics is large and complex. It is not difficult to understand, providing sufficient interest is taken to find out what is involved. To this end, the reader will find a list of points which give a reasonable background to this most absorbing aspect of collecting. The details of this chapter have been restricted to information on three aspects. These are: (a) what intending competitors need to know about; (b) background information which other collectors, who have no strong interest in internationals, may wish to learn of; (c) information helpful to the general public visiting such an exhibition.

With this in mind, and for ease of reading, certain extracts from the general and the thematic rules, as set out in the bulletin referred to earlier, have been made and these will also be found in Appendix F.

At the exhibition
Internationals are very large events and sometimes require the use of a number of buildings to house all the exhibits. The seeming miles of frames, all of the same pattern, and the numbering arrangement of them can easily produce a sense of bewilderment. Whether you are an exhibitor or not, it may be useful to know about these large shows as regards the kind of exhibits which are on show and the way to look at them. Both of these are important if the visit to the exhibition is to be enjoyable. Even more important, however, is the matter of how to best spend your time there.

THE EXHIBITS

1   In the court of honour. Here collections of notable persons or of particular interest are shown on the special invitation of the organising committee of the exhibition. They are not shown for competitive purposes but, because they are of such outstanding merit, special effort should be made to see at least those in the thematic part.

2   The official class is also non-competitive and comprises the participation by postal administrations, postal museums, printers and designers. Much unusual material is put on show in this class, but it is often of general rather than thematic interest.

3   There are generally three other classes of non-competitive exhibit. These are: (a) exhibits by members of the jury; (b) the 'hors concours' class for displays owned by collectors who are not allowed or do not wish to be in a competitive class; (c) the class of honour reserved for collections which have been awarded a total of three large gold medals at previous

internationals. These three groups always contain much excellent material and use should be made of the catalogue to locate and see any of a thematic nature.

4   The competitive classes comprise by far the greater part of the exhibition. Because they are large and have a wide range of material, examining this section of the show frequently causes much confusion and over-exertion. With these points in mind, the following notes may be of value to the visitor to the exhibition.

The description of the competitive exhibits as shown in the catalogue usually occupies a considerable number of pages. With allowances for the differences between one exhibition and another, the order in the catalogue generally corresponds to the following pattern.

(a)   Two or more classes for the stamps of the country in which the exhibition is being held. These account for a considerable proportion of the exhibits.
(b)   Postal history and pre-philately.
(c)   Thematic and subject collections.
(d)   Airmails.
(e)   Postal stationery and other sorts of collections.
(f)   Junior collections.
(g)   Literature.

Besides making an examination of the exhibits in the thematic and subject classes, opportunity should be taken to examine those in the literature and junior classes for information sources or material which will be of value to the collector.

AWARDS
There are two types of award, grand prix (which generally consist of art objects) and medals. These latter range from large-sized gold medals at the top, small gold, gilded silver, silver, silver-plated bronze and lastly bronze medals. The level of award made in each case can be usefully regarded as the measure of exhibition merit, in terms of the judging criteria, of an entry and the minimum requirement for the levels of award is given on page 147.

LOOKING AT THEMATICS AS A VISITOR

As a visitor and not an exhibitor, for you it is a matter of enjoyment first, appreciation next and education thereafter, always providing that the latter is something which you also enjoy and require. Not all people who visit large exhibitions find them entirely to their liking, mainly because the tendency to wander from frame to frame looking half-heartedly at the exhibits can very easily produce tiredness and even exhaustion. The secret of a successful visit to an international runs along these lines. Immediately you have the catalogue, take about 5–10 minutes to see how it is made up, in so far as the exhibits are concerned. Then mark up the details of the entries you think you would like to see. If you have the help of an experienced friend, so much the better. Then also mark the location of these exhibits on the plan of the exhibition and work out a system of seeing what you want rather than haphazardly. A word about your 'experienced friend' may save a little difficulty. Try not to enlist the services of one who, creditably enough, considers it to be his duty to convert you to this or that subject which, of course, is his own collecting interest. As a non-competitor you are thoroughly entitled to think whatever you like about the exhibits and to say what seems reasonable to you about them. But, above all, decide that exhibitions are enjoyable.

FOR THE EXHIBITOR OR INTENDING EXHIBITOR

Your focus, of course, is quite different from that of the average type of visitor mentioned previously. One of your main objectives is to secure the satisfaction which comes from increased knowledge and wider experience. There is also the reassuring effect which results from being able to see your work alongside that of others, not only at the same level as your own, but also both above and below it. This establishes confidence, enabling you to make decisions and resolutions and these very human processes are the starting points of progress.

Here is your viewing angle. Gazing at the gold-medal entries one after another may be exciting, but it is not a very constructive exercise; in some circumstances it can be decidedly discouraging and even humiliating. Neither is of any real value to the collector looking for practical advice. The better method of seeing the thematic exhibits is to plan to enjoy seeing a limited number as a contrasting process. To spend a reasonable amount of time making this systematic contrast in terms of merit is really far more valuable than just appreciating that 'this is certainly a gold-medal exhibit', or a little later on deciding at a glance that 'this one deserves its silver award'.

This exercise must be done to a practical plan. When the catalogue has been obtained, decide there and then that the dividends for you lie in the careful examination of the exhibits in the thematic class.

If you are a starter collector, perhaps it would be wise to appreciate that gold-medal entries can very well make strong discouraging impressions on you. So avoid them until the really valuable bit, the comparison exercise, has been done. Mark in the catalogue the frame numbers of, say, six exhibits which have secured a silver award and then a corresponding number which have obtained a bronze.

If you have in mind the preparation of a subject exhibit then select the two groups of (about) six frame numbers from subject collections on view. Similarly, if you hope to submit a theme type of entry, mark up theme submissions. Begin this contrast exercise by an examination of the exhibits in the upper (silver) level and try to get a clear impression of the main characteristics running through them. After that, examine the selected entries which have won a bronze medal, but making a particular point of isolating the feature differences between these and the companion entries in the upper level.

Which points to look for and to contrast? Here are some: (a) the care with which the introductory sheets have been prepared and their effectiveness vis-à-vis the material in the entry; (b) the style and the care with which the stamps, covers etc. have been presented; (c) the types and amounts of material used (a wide range of items is listed in the earlier chapters of the book); (d) the clarity with which the stamps tell the story of the theme or illustrate the steps in the subject; now for a most important item (e) the evidence of a logical progression over the whole of the entry. Here are some negative checks: (f) that no items of a collateral or non-philatelic nature have been included; (g) that no sheet is overcrowded when considered by international exhibition standards. This is important for you to get into the right perspective. Generally, between nationals and internationals, there is considerable difference in the spacing of stamps. In internationals, where the stamp's undoubtedly the thing (unless a postal-history type of exhibit is involved), spacing between items must be generous, and the balance above reproach. Last, (h) that no stamps or sheets on the FIP harmful or undesirable lists (black blot items in the USA) have been included.

Do not hurry over this contrast exercise and discuss each point fully with your colleague so that when you are ready to leave the exhibition, the pictures in your mind are as complete as possible. When you come to start on your entry begin by making an honest estimate of the strength of your material and your ability. Set your sights a little higher than your first estimate and you will then have an ambitious target to aim at.

Perhaps you are a competitor in this or in a previous international. If so, making the contrasts suggested previously may well be even more valuable to you. It would be useful to use the award which your entry has already secured at the lower level and make the comparisons with, say, one or two levels higher. But, if a silver medal is already in your possession, some thinking needs to be done. Here is a point which may be new to you. In awarding medals at internationals, according to the regulations, the following grading applies:

Medals	Lowest points secured	
Large gold	95	
Gold	90	5 points
Vermeil	85	5 points
Silver	75	10 points
Silver-plated bronze	60	15 points
Bronze	50	10 points

(Note: vermeil is an alternative description for gilded silver)

It will be noted that the largest step by far (15 points) is between the silver-plated bronze and the silver medals. What is far more important, however, is that the grading between 95 at the top and 50 at the bottom, with the uneven steps for the intermediate awards, does not, in practice, seem to represent the amount of exhibition merit for each step. *Illustration 11.1* shows the five steps according to the number of points secured. A survey of the awards made over a number of exhibitions suggests that the increases in exhibition merit are not clearly related to the figures of the points secured as given previously. In fact, the author suggests that a more realistic picture like that of *Illustration 11.2* applies. In practice, this means that the higher up the scale you get, the greater is the amount of merit which your material must exhibit to attain one step more. In short, the higher, the harder. Wisely, therefore, make your comparison exercise with care, bearing in mind that increases in time, money and expertise will be needed if you are to go forward. As an experienced thematic exhibitor with the benefit of a good knowledge of internationals, you should find the contrasting exercise suggested here to be not only enjoyable but instructive as well.

SOME 'DONT'S' FOR EXHIBITORS

First, make a particular point of not including any non-philatelic (or collateral) material, however attractive or expensive in the entry. Very occasionally you may consider that a small discreet map would be useful to help the explanation. As a general rule, unless the inclusion is absolutely essential, it is better to leave it out. Next, make a check that none of the material it is proposed to exhibit is included in the FIP list of harmful or undesirable issues. Guessing whether this or that stamp is in the list is not very wise, so make a point of getting a copy of these documents. If necessary, an enquiry of the commissioner appointed for your country may help. In America, the equivalent is the black blot list issued by the Amercan Philatelic Society. Another very important point too is that, in thematics and subject entries, the use of used stamps is to be avoided unless they are for the purpose of showing a cancellation.

TWO OUT OF MANY

The international area of exhibiting is a very large and important one. However, there are many collectors who have no direct interest in the many details which the exhibitor would regard as vital. Space allows for only two of these to be dealt with in this chapter. These are (a) the introductory sheets for a theme exhibit and for a subject exhibit, and (b) the judging criteria for each of these types of entry.

THE THEMATIC EXHIBIT AND PLAN OR INTRODUCTION
The following have been extracted from the international rules of the FIP (1977).

Article 1   The thematic collection develops a theme or illustrates an idea following a logical plan, using the motives offered by the stamps, as well as the information supplied by the philatelic or postal documents. Therefore, the stamps and documents shall be in strict relation to the theme or idea selected.

For the exhibitor, the teeth of this definition are at two points: in the vital phrase 'following a logical plan' and in the last sentence. Failure to keep these in mind may well mean that these teeth will take their toll. Now for the introductory plan (for a thematic exhibit).

Article 2   The plan of the collection, presented as a preface, must be logical and correct and will supply the necessary information, including the divisions to estimate the size of the collection. A precise and accurate text must clearly indicate the development of the theme.

Note the point that the preface describes the entry and not the historical, scientific or sociological background which may be highly interesting but is largely irrelevant from the judging aspect. The plan has two important jobs to do. The first is to describe the general idea behind the arrangement of the collection. In other words, what it sets out to show. This description should commence with a short, clear explanation contained within three or four lines at the most, and designed in the simplest of terms to give the judges a clear understanding of the idea of the exhibit. This should be followed by a breakdown of the entry into the main facets, with the number of sheets in each, in the order in which they will be found in the exhibit. It is wise to cover at least those sections which carry the greatest thematic weight; for the sake of clarity omit the minor details.

The other important function is to give a precise and accurate description of the development. This means that each of the principal steps in the exhibit, in the order in which the judges will find them, should be clearly described in such a way as to show the linkage between them. Identify the starting point, in terms of the title, and also give the reason why the commencement at this point has been so selected. Then give the major steps by which the story of the theme unfolds, leading from one aspect to the next until the end is reached. This must tally exactly with what is shown on the sheets. It is unwise to attempt to cover any weaknesses in the logical development by inaccuracies, overstatements or loose generalities. It is unreasonable to expect the judges to have confidence in the entry when the preface describes an attractive exhibit, the sheets of which fail to come up to the expectations. Here is a point which does not arise in national exhibitions. The accepted languages are English and French and the preface should therefore be given in both. If the exhibition is in an English-speaking country, then the order is, of course, the English version followed by the French. In all other countries, reverse this order, introducing the heading as the 'exposé' or 'preface'. If languages are not your strong point, go to an expert and get the right translation. It is very helpful if he is also a collector as this will allow the correct equivalents of your English terminology to be used. To exhibit your laxity right at the start of the exhibit is not a good way to begin so don't be tempted to guess anything.

THE SUBJECT EXHIBIT

Article 6   The subject collection includes all postage stamps and philatelic documents related to the subject or purpose of issue. The presentation of the material can be in a systematic, thematic order and/or by country and chronological order.

Here the focal point for the exhibitor is the last sentence. The general arrangement of a systematic entry can be seen from the example in Appendix B, 'Bird Life', whilst the idea behind a chronological type of exhibit is shown in Appendix E under the title 'The Life and Works of William Shakespeare'.

THE PLAN OF THE SUBJECT COLLECTION

Article 8   The Subject collection must be preceded by a plan which introduces the material displayed, illustrates the criteria followed in its realisation and gives an idea of the extent of the collection and the development of the different parts.

As in the case of the theme exhibit preface, the introduction to the subject must avoid anything in the shape of an essay covering the background to the subject generally. Any information of this sort should be restricted to that which it is essential the judges know about, if they are to deal fairly with the exhibit. At the start, give a short, clear explanation of what your title involves, using the simplest words possible. This expansion of the title can then logically be followed by a more detailed explanation linked to a description of the material which is on show. This latter phase of the preface is the point at which the functions of the groups of stamps, covers etc. are shown to be integral parts of the subject. It is therefore a practical description. Since it deals with a large range of material, care must be taken not to produce a long, wordy single paragraph. So, highlight in words the main groups of material, but mention any rarities or other special pieces. If there are any important points which have had to be covered by out-of-the-way material, then explain the reasons why this has been done.

How to explain 'the criteria followed in its realisation'? In ordinary usage, the criteria are the standards by which a judgement is made or an estimate is obtained. In thematic terms this means the reasons why you are showing the subject your way; why you have 'gone to town' on certain aspects and not on others; why you see some as more important than others. Of course, the exhibit must correspond to what you have written: that is essential. The real aim of this section, by explaining why this and why that has been done, is to get the judges in the same thinking area as you. Then they can fully appreciate your efforts before forming an idea of the merit of the exhibit. The more honest you are with yourself about the preface, the more likely it is that you will take the judges along with you and the better will be their appraisal of your entry.

Lastly, you may like to know the following:

Article 12   The presentation of the collection must be clean, neat and present a harmonious entity.

What this means in practice can be properly appreciated only by a visit to at least two international exhibitions.

THE JUDGING CRITERIA
The rules of the FIP (slightly rearranged to save space) state:

Article 13   In evaluating the collections, the jury will observe the following criteria:

Criterion	Theme	Subject
	Maximum points	
1 Presentation and general impression	10	10
2 Philatelic knowledge	15	20
3 Condition and rarity of the stamps and documents	25	30
4 Plan of the collection and development of the theme	20	—
5 Originality and setting-up of the theme	25	—
6 Size of the collection	5	—
7 Systematic study and size of the collection	—	25
8 Setting up the subject	—	15
	100	100

It is essential to note that the judging criteria as set out in the regulations are not the sole yardstick by which the merits of the exhibits are assessed. The general impression of the exhibit is included in the criteria which are in the nature of a general guide to the judges. Of necessity, the other factors likely to be taken into account must be intangible. Possibly that most likely to influence them is the clear appearance of signs that the exhibitor has not only a very creditable knowledge of the theme/subject, but also has exercised his ability to the maximum and so produced an outstanding entry. 'Outstanding' does not mean full of rarities or philatelic 'tricks' or the like. The nearest that the author can get to this rather elusive requirement is that the exhibit, in its stamps and covers etc., tells the story of the theme or shows the subject far better and more compellingly than any arrangement of words. The picture produced by the entry is so clear and attractive that it outshines any oral or verbal description.

Another point to note is that originality is only of importance in the theme collection. Also bear in mind that rarity has now to be included in both the subject and the theme exhibits. Very few nationals take account of rarity and an entry in one of these competitions is often very well placed despite the fact that none of the stamps etc. comes into the category of rarity. Unless care is taken to re-arrange the exhibit to show a good proportion of rare stamps, the submission to an international will usually result in a loss of marks. The inclusion of philatelic knowledge as one of the criteria certainly justifies some explanation of the meaning of this term:

Article 11 The presence and variety of the various philatelic elements (stamps, covers, cancellations, handstamps, postal stationery, etc.) will allow the assessment of the collector's philatelic knowledge. These items must be authentic and in good condition. The cancellations should be neat and cover the stamps as little as possible. The FIPs decisions concerning harmful or undesirable issues will be applied. Non-philatelic items cannot, in principle, be admitted.

The intending exhibitor should note carefully the intent of the last two sentences. Not even a single item which offends these two conditions should be allowed in the collection.

Now for two final thoughts. The theme entry, if it is to do well, must present a development which positively shines: it should be so strong and clear that it cannot be missed. On the other hand, the subject exhibit must impress because of the depth to which it has been studied and represented in the collection. Because of its importance in international exhibitions, it is essential to appreciate to the full the extent of the difference between a theme and a subject exhibit as expressed previously. Care and attention to this aspect when preparing the entry can make a considerable difference to the results.

12 Selling the Collection

If you decide to sell your collection, the line of action is roughly as follows. First, it is most important to put all the collection and any stockbooks into apple-pie order. The pages of the collection should be in the correct sequence with as few as possible blank spaces on them and there should be no loose stamps, odd pieces of paper, etc. lying between the leaves. Any effort you make to put the collection into a clean and presentable condition will be to your advantage in due course. All the surplus material should be arranged in country/catalogue order so that it can be seen and handled easily. It is also useful to make up separately all 'good' items from the cash angle.

When all these steps have been completed, and not before, consult the dealer, auctioneer or other sales outlet of your choice. Make a special appointment and undertake the journey to do this as well, rather than arrive out-of-the-blue. Do try to listen carefully to the advice offered, especially if it is clear at the outset that your collection does not impress the dealer because nothing helps to foster seller/buyer confidence so much as sincerity. Unless you are in a hurry and do not mind what this may cost you, allow the prospective purchaser plenty of time to go over the collection in order to appreciate precisely what it contains. It is useful to have a very approximate figure in mind to which you would say 'Yes, thank you' or alternatively 'Well, thanks for looking at it, but I did have a rather higher figure in mind.' A little experience in this area of selling is always of very considerable value.

Above all, keep in mind that both aspects of the hobby, buying and selling, can be equally pleasant experiences for you and that as many pleasant friendships are frequently made whilst selling as when buying.

Appendix

A   Short list of subjects
Notes:

1   This is not a list of all the subjects which can be formed into a collection.
2   It comprises those subjects about which sufficient information has already been published to allow the setting-up and development of a reasonably complete collection to be made.
3   The addition of (vwb) and (wb) after a subject indicates that it is classified as Very Wide Band or Wide Band respectively. In these cases it is usual for collections to be concentrated on one or a group of parts rather than on the whole subject.

Africana
Aircraft
Americana (vwb)
Angling
Animals (wb)
Antarctica
Art and artists (wb)
Art Galleries
Astronomy
Atomic Energy
Authors
Automotive Industry
Aviation (wb)

Banks
Bible

Biology
Birds (wb)
Books
Botany
Bridges
Buildings
Butterflies

Canals
Cats
Cattle
Carvings
Ceramics
Chemistry

Chess

155

Philosophers
Physics
Plants
Poetry
Polar life
Police
Politics
Printing

Radio and TV
Railways (wb)
Recreation
Red Cross
Religion (wb)
Revenue stamps
Rivers
Rockets
Rotary
Royalty (vwb)

Science
Scouts and Guides
Sculpture

Ships (vwb)
Snakes and reptiles
Space (vwb)
Sport (wb)
Stamp artists

Tapestry
Textiles
Theatre
Transportation (wb)
Trees

Umbrellas
United Nations (wb)
The Universal Postal Union

War
Watercraft
Waterfalls
Welfare
World fairs

Zoology

B Make-up of a subject collection with the title 'Bird Life'
Comments:

1   This collector is an active bird watcher with a scientific background and has an excellent working knowledge of ornithology. Thus, Part 4 (World distribution) with 9 sections has 71 subsidiary parts and reflects the collector's background. In short, the motto is 'science with a story'.
2   The figures in parentheses show the number of subsidiary parts in each case.
3   The number of subsidiary parts is not always indicative of the size of each group of parts, thus Part 5 (Birds of my home area) is treated as a single subject but occupies about 100 pages of the 650 page collection.

Part 1   Evolution
  (a) Language (6)
  (b) Nesting habits (12)
  (c) Foods and feeding (13)
  (d) Flight

Part 2   Flight (4)

Part 3   Migration (8)

Part 4   World distribution
  (a) Eurasia (13)
  (b) N. America (17)
  (c) S. America (6)
  (d) Africa (7)
  (e) S. Asia (8)
  (f) Australasia (12)
  (g) Islands (2)
  (h) Antarctica (5)
  (i) World distribution of parrots

Part 5   Birds of my home area
  This part of the collection is arranged on a geographical basis and is often used for talks to local societies.

Part 6   Birds and man
  (a) Birds of religion (3)
  (b) Birds of legend (1)
  (c) Birds in art and literature (5)
  (d) Birds as symbols (6)
  (e) Birds for pleasure (3)
  (f) Birds for food (13)
  (g) Birds for sport (3)
  (h) Utilisation of birds (3)
  (i) Bird pests (3)

Part 7   Conservation (4)

Part 8   Extinct birds (1)

C   Make-up of a subject collection with the title 'Textiles'
Comments:

1   This collector has a very good educational background in the arts, ballet and costume and is currently a craftsman in textile design. Much of this work has been included in international exhibitions. The textile thematic collection is now almost complete as are the parallel collections on ballet and dance.

2   The list shown below has been constructed to show only the main groupings. Each of these contains a number of subsidiary parts.

3   As is usual with subject collections, there is a considerable overlap between the divisions as shown in this list.

Part 1   Sources
  (a) Plants
  (b) Trees
  (c) Animals
  (d) Chemicals
  (e) Minerals

Part 2   Raw materials
  (a) Cotton
  (b) Wool
  (c) Silk
  (d) Hair
  (e) Artificial fibres
  (f) Hemp, sisal, etc.
  (g) Minerals

Part 3   Processes
  (a) Hand-spinning
  (b) Wheel-spinning
  (c) Loom-weaving
  (d) Tapestry-weaving
  (e) Lace, needle and bobbin
  (f) Knitting
  (g) Crochet
  (h) Macramé

(i) Felting
(j) Dyes

Part 4   Uses
(a) Household fabrics
(b) Commercial fabrics
(c) Wearing apparel
(d) Special costumes including national, local, royal and ecclesiastical
(e) Heraldic

Part 5   Ornamentation
(a) Surface decoration
(b) Embroidery
(c) Wall coverings
(d) Knots
(e) Metallic threads

Part 6   Stitches
(a) National
(b) Local

Part 7   Ancient uses
(a) Ancient history
(b) Folklore
(c) Legend
(d) Symbolic

D   Notes on a theme collection 'The Work of the Stamp Designer, Miss Jennifer Toombs'
Comments:

1   The owner–collection relationship in this example is radically different from those of the three previous in this Appendix.
2   The collector is an electrical engineer of considerable standing, mature, well-balanced, but confesses to no creative ability in art.
3   The selection of this subject by the owner was a matter of accident. Some years ago he was attracted by the clarity and

directness of the designs of four stamps. Liking the style he decided to concentrate on collecting more of this stamp designer's work.

4   The collection was initially set up on a geographical basis, but currently it has been re-arranged more satisfactorily on a chronological one.

5   This is a typical example of the selection by a collector of a subject quite remote from his general life interests. It therefore falls in the personal category of collections.

Part 1   Introduction

Part 2   This covers the arrangement of each group of designs in chronological order
  (a) Stamps only by the designer
  (b) Both cover and stamp by the designer
  (c) Cover only by the designer
      1   FDC
      2   Special event
      3   Charity
  (d) Other covers with stamps by the designer
  (e) Air letters
  (f) Booklets
  (g) Presentation packs
  (h) Associated artwork
  (i) Publicity material

The current size of the collection is approximately 350 sheets.

Part E   Make-up of a theme collection 'The Life and Works of William Shakespeare'
Comments:

1   This collector has a well-balanced, serious outlook with an interest in history. He likes practical and analytical ways of handling problems such as the assembly of this collection.

2   The method of approach, which has a historical flavour, is typical of that required for early historical subjects where the complete chronological sequence is not known at the beginning.

3   As a whole, the collection presents a somewhat disconnected pattern as far as the works of William Shakespeare are concerned. Competitive entries drawn from it, however, secured several high awards.

4   The collector appreciated that there was a need for good linkage between each section of the part covering the plays. Good use was made of narrative matter to bind the whole of this part together and thus improve the story generally.

Notes on method of approach:

1   Shakespeare commenced his writing with the Poems and Sonnets. The precise year during which he wrote many of his 35 plays has not yet been settled, but four groups of plays have been fairly firmly fixed. The Romances are thought to have been written between 1609 and his death in 1616. The groups established so far are 1592 (four plays), 1595 (4), 1594–1600 (4) and 1600–4 (6).

2   The work of relating stamps and plays makes use of these four periods in the first instance. The Romances and the balance of the plays then follow as the next two aspects of his works.

3   Because the types of plays—the Histories, Tragedies, Comedies and Romances—were not written in groups at specific dates, an arrangement on this basis would not have satisfied the historical bent of the owner.

4   The following list served as a guide during the location of suitable stamps and covers to illustrate the plays of Shakespeare, his early life and the many commemorative stamps and cancellations which have appeared:

1   Introduction (or prologue)
2   Elizabethan England
3   Birthplace
4   Early life
5   Youth and marriage
6   Plays of about 1592
7   Plays of about 1594
8   Plays in the period 1594–1600
9   Plays in the period 1600–1604

10 The Romances, 1609–16
11 The rest of the plays
12 The death of Shakespeare
13 The 1964 omnibus issues and cancels
14 Birthday cancels
15 Other cancels
16 Shakespeare in the modern style
17 Place name cancels, festival and other cancels
18 Epilogue

Part F   The following extracts from the thematic rules of the FIP, which have not already been reproduced in this book, may be of use to the exhibitor

Thematic collections
Article 3   The originality of the Theme will be treated meticulously. The collection will be enhanced by careful research made by the collector, allowing his personality to be brought forth.

Article 4   The size of the collection will allow a clear and complete development of the proposed theme.

Subject collections
Article 8   The subject collection must be accompanied by a clear and concise descriptive text. Its only function is to comment on the systematic development and the own features of the collection.

Article 9   The development of the subject collection requires deep philatelic research of the chosen subject or purpose of the issue.

General
Article 15   In an International Exhibition, 5 frames at least shall be at the disposal of the collector allowing him to show the development of the collection plan and present the interesting philatelic items.

Bibliography

1   The two books by Charles E. Foster on the general aspects of stamp collecting recommended in Chapter 8, *How to Prepare Stamp Exhibits* and *Showcasing Your Collection*, can be obtained from: Hobby Publishing Services, 1318 7th Street, NW, Albuquerque, New Mexico, NM 87102, USA or Vera Trinder Ltd, 38 Bedford Street, Strand, London WC2E 9EU.

2   The information in this bibliography is arranged to cover publications by the American Topical Association as one group in subject order and relates only to published books and not articles appearing in periodicals.

3   The American Topical Association publications. Part A of the Appendix to this book gives a list of 138 general classifications of subjects. This corresponds exactly to the General Index issued by the ATA and covering both handbooks and articles in *Topical Time*, the journal of the association. Each single listing in Part A represents a section of the ATA publications list which details some 2,500 separate titles covering the handbooks (HB) and the articles. The list, '1979–80 Topical Stamp Publications' and which is also the ordering form, can be obtained from The American Topical Association, 3308 North 50th Street, Milwaukee, Wisconsin 53216, USA.

4   ATA handbooks (HB):

World Jets on Stamps by DeMars (HB 57); *Americana on Foreign Stamps,* 2 vols by Wagner (HB 58 & 85); *Astronomy and Philately* by the Astro Study Unit (HB 90); *Birds of the World on Stamps,* by Stanley, Ridgley and Eglais (HB 82); *Cooking with Stamps* by Brooks (HB 56); *Drugs and Pharmacy on Stamps* by Griffenhagen (HB 55); *Education on Stamps* by Brooks (HB 68); *Europa on Stamps* by the Europa Study Unit (HB 34); *Fairy*

Tales and Folk Tales on Stamps by Partington (HB 73); *Family on Stamps* by Norris, Christmas Study Unit (HB 92); *Fishes, Amphibia and Reptiles of the World* by Bearse, Stanley, Baasch, Bockwalter, Gordon and Scaroff (HB 91); *Flowers on Stamps* by Patterson (HB 61); *Horses on Stamps* by Wetmore (HB 52); *Holy Family on Stamps* by Morris (HB 92); *Kennedy, John F., Stamps of the World* by Green and Czesany (HB 50); *Lions International on Stamps* by Dekom (HB 50); *Mammals of the World on Stamps* by Wagner (HB 79); *Masonic Stamps of the World* by Beltman (HB 43); *Medical History in Philately* by Newerla (HB 39); *Medical Stamps by Hainlen* (HB 63); *Private Die Proprietary Medicine Stamps* by Griffenhagen (HB 66); *Medicine Tax Stamps World Wide* by Griffenhagen (HB 76); *Music World of Stamps* by Whitehead (HB 84); *Nudes, Philatelic* by Deane (HB 53); *Old Glory Around the World* by Burkley and Dockall (HB 75); *Plants on Stamps* by Delfeld, Sents and Patterson (HB 94); *Railway Stamps* by Burkhalter and Wales (HB 77); *Religion on Stamps, History* by Norse (HB 36); *Roosevelt, Eleanor and Franklin D.* by Silver and Bart (HB 48); *Science Stamps* by Truman (HB 87); *Space Covers* by Peters (HB 60); *Sports and Recreation* by Bruce (HB 83); *Stamps on Stamps, Centenaries* by Leland (HB 45); *Theatre Philatelic* by Shiffler (HB 67); *United Nations Stamps of the World* by Parkin (HB 51); *US History as Portrayed by US Stamps* by Tasker (HB 51); *Watercraft on Stamps* by Herd (HB 80); *Women on Stamps*, vol. 1 by Webb (HB 71), vol. 2 by Killingbeck (HB 93).

Thematic/topical publications

AEROPLANES

Aerogrammes by Peter Jennings, published by Picton Publishing, Bath Road, Chippenham, Wilts; *Catalogue of Aerogrammes of the World* by Frank Muller, Paris, 1950; *Catalogue Mondialles Entiers Aeropostaux* by François Godinas, 1967; *Jack Knight Air Log*, published by Aerophilatelic Federation of the Americas, USA; *Kesslers Catalogue of Aerogrammes*, 3 vols, published by Lava, New York; *Stamps and Aircraft* by James Watson, published by Faber & Faber, London, 1961; *Saga of the Civil Mail* by Carrol V. Clines, published by D. Van Nostrand, London; *California on US Stamps* by Francis J. Weber, published by the author, Worcester, Mass., USA, 1975; *United*

States Stamps by Harvey R. Warm, published by Scott Publishing Co., New York, 1977.

ARCHERY
Archery by Carlo Condarelli (in English and Italian) from the author, 95129 Catania, Italy.

ARCTIC AND ANTARCTIC
Antarctic Posts and Stamps by J. B. Harvey Pirie, London, 1975; *Polar Explorations* by Eric E. Wise, London, 1976; 'Postal History of the Antarctic 1904–48', published in *The Polar Record*, No. 41, Jan. 1951.

ART AND ARTISTS
Artists and Art by Thomas V. Varsky, published by the TV Philatelic Co., New York, 11352; *Maestros Catalogue of Stamps Reproducing Paintings* by Balasse and Regiter, Brussels, 1968; *Paintings on Stamps,* catalogues by J. Balasse, Brussels; *Portraits on Stamps* by Fredrik Arsenius, published Stockholm, 1930.

ATOMIC ENERGY
Stamps Tell the Story of Nuclear Energy by Joseph J. Angelo Jr, published by the US Energy and Development Administration, Washington, USA.

BICYCLES
Bicycles and the Postage Stamp by R. F. Sudbury, published by Hughes, 1976.

BIRDS
Bird Stamps of the World, checklist by Hugh Lant, published by the author, Hull; *Bird Names on Stamps* in English and German (scientific) by Herbert von Timmerman, Bremen, Germany; *Birds of the World as found on Postage Stamps* by Sidney R. Ester, published by Grosse & Dunlap, USA; *Collect Birds on Stamps* by Christine E. Jackson, published by H. F. and G. Witherby, London; *Duck Stamp Data,* published by US Bureau of Sports and Wild Life, Washington, USA.

BOYS BRIGADE
Boys Brigade Stamps and Postmarks by Stanley K. Hunter, published by the author, Glasgow, 1977.

BUTTERFLIES AND MOTHS
Butterflies and Moths on Stamps by G. J. Barber, published by the author, Surrey, 1977.

CHESS
Chess on Stamps by Peter C. Burnett, published by Picton Publishing, Bath Road, Chippenham, Wilts.

CHRISTMAS
Christmas Story by Mary Mansfield, published by the Guild of St Gabriel, Wallington, Surrey; *Christmas in Advance* by Meredith and Kidd, published by Robson Lowe Ltd, London, 1974; *Seventy-Five Years of Christmas Stamps* by Walter A. Sage and Kathleen M. Bing, published by COROS, Tucson, Arizona 28504.

CHRISTIANITY
Bible Through Stamps by Ord Malek, published by Ktva Hara Publishing, New York; *Brief Biographies of Protestant Personalities on Stamps* by Rev. E. J. A. Marxhausen and Lee Kleinhans, published by the authors, USA; *Catalogue of Marian Stamps* by W. J. Hoffman, published by Marian Philatelic Study Group, Orange, California, USA; *Catalogue of Modonna Stamps, Spanish Civil War*, by Marshall H. Williams, published by Marian Philatelic Study Group as previous; *Catholica on Amercan Stamps* by Francis J. Weber, published by Hillside Press, Titton, USA; *Postage Stamps and the Bible Story* by Alfred E. Gould, published by Marshall, Morgan & Scott, London, 1968; *Postage Stamps and Christianity* by Barbara R. Mueller, published by Concordia Publishing House, Missouri, USA.

CHURCHILL
Churchill on Stamps by James A. Mackay, published by the author, Amersham, Bucks; *Churchill Collectors' Handbook*, published by the International Churchill Society, Farnborough, Hants.

COLUMBUS
Columbus by Dr J. H. van Peursen, published by Philatelie en Geschiedebis, Holland.

COOKING
Cooking by Ruth S. Webster, published by Philatelic Cook Books, N. Mexico, Philatelic Association, USA.

DANCE
Ballet Dancing and Dance Checklist by Luise R. Mecmski and Dr John S. Papa, published by Fine Arts Philatelist, Midland, Michigan 48640, USA.

ELECTRONICS
'Electronics Industry on Stamps' by M. W. Martin, published in *Electronics and Power*, May 1973.

ENTOMOLOGY
Butterflies and Moths on Stamps by Clifford S. Baker, published by BLSC Publishing Co., London, 1976; *Insects on Stamps*, checklist, by F. G. A. M. Smit, published by author in Tring, Herts; *Postage Stamps Showing Bees and Hives* by K. F. Preuss, published by the Bee Research Association, Bucks.

EUROPA
Europa Stamps Catalogue, published by Edouard Berck, Paris, 1962.

FISH AND WILDLIFE
Fish and Wildlife Service USA, published by Superintendent of Documents, Government Printing Office, Washington, USA, 1969.

FLOWERS
La Flore by Clement Brun, published by Brun et Fils, Paris, 1967.

JUDAICA
International-Judaica Philatelic Handbook, published by SAR Academy, Riverside, New York.

LAW
Lawyers on Stamps by G. S. Ryan, published by the author, Northwood, Middlesex.

LIBRARIES
Catalogue of Libraries on Stamps by IFLA Netherex Bibliothek, The Hague, Holland.

MAPS

Studies in Postal Cartography by Walter Klinefelter, published by Sunac Press, La Crosse, USA, 1978.

MASONS

Masonic Philately by Sam Brooks, published by the Masonic Stamp Club, New York; *Masonic Stamp Collection* by George B. Clark, published by Masonic Service Association, Washington, USA.

MEDICINE

The Philatelic Herbalist by Tom King, published by C.H.R. Parsons, London, 1961; *Medicine Told by Stamps* by Erik Ak-Upmark, published by Almquist & Wilkser, Stockholm, 1976; *Philatelic Medicine*, published by Allisa Stamps Inc., Wilmington, Delaware, USA; *Medical History in Philately* by Gerhard A. Newerla, published Waltham, Mass., USA; *Medicine and Stamps* by R. A. Kyle and M. A. Shampo, published by the Chicago and American Medical Association.

METHODISM

Methodist Stamps and Postmarks by John Thomas Aungiers, published by Methodist Philatelic Society, Cheshire, England; *Methodism in the South Pacific* by Methodist Philatelic, published as previous.

MUSIC

The Baton, Journal of the Philatelic Music Circle, published from Cardiff CF4 1PE; *Beethoven in the Stamp Album*, published by the Philatelic Music Circle as previous; *Check List of Stamps about Music* by A. H. R. Grimsey, published by the National Philatelic Society, London; *Music on Stamps* (in 6 parts) by Sylvester Peat, published by the Picton Publishing Co., Bath Road, Chippenham, Wilts, England; *Stamps and Music* by James Watson, published by Faber & Faber, London; *Musical Instruments, Opera* and *Music and Musicians*, checklist, published by the Fine Arts Philatelist, Midland, Michigan 48640, USA.

MYTHOLOGY

Postage Stamps and Greek Mythology by H. Gordon Harris, published by Harris Publications Ltd, London, 1932.

NATURAL HISTORY
Natural History on Stamps by James H. Lyons, published by the
New England Stamp Co., 1936.

OLYMPIC GAMES
A Philatelic History of the Olympic Games, by Ernest Trory,
published by the Crabtree Press, Brighton, Sussex, 1956.
History and Vignettes of 1932 Olympic Games by Sherwin
Podolstoy, published by Sports Philatelic International,
California, USA; *Catalogue of Olympic Games* by J. Augflaget &
Sieger Verlag, Württemberg.

PRINTING
Printers and Printing in Philately by John Alden, published by
the Picton Press, Bath Road, Chippenham, Wilts.

RAILWAYS
Railways on Stamps, 3 vols, by A. U. Goodbody, published by
Picton Publishing, Bath Road, Chippenham, Wilts; *Stamps and
Railways* by James M. C. Watson, published by Faber &
Faber, London, 1962; *List of Stamps associated with Railways*,
2nd edn, by R. D. Cornish, published by the Railway Philatelic
Group; *The Railway Theme, Railways and Stamps* by Charles A.
Hart, published by the Railway Philatelic Group, 1970.

RELIGION
Religion on Stamps by Waller A. Sagar and Kathleen M. Bing,
published by COROS, Tucson, Arizona, USA.

ROYALTY
The Stamp of Royalty (1935–72) by A. C. Rigo de Righi,
published by the National Postal Museum, London; *Stamp
Portraits of the Queen* by Cyril R. H. Parsons, published by
Stanley Gibbons Ltd, London, 1959.

SCOUTS AND GUIDES
Boy Scout and Girl Guide Stamps of the World by Gordon
Entwhistle, published by Cassell, London, 1957. *Catalogue of
Scout and Guide Stamps of the World* by A. N. Nicholson,
published by Howard L. Fears, Seaford, Sussex; *Scout*

Personalities on Stamps by Stanley K. Hunter, published by the author, Glasgow, 1973.

SHIPS
Ships on Stamps, Parts 1–8 by Ernest W. Argyle, published by Picton Publishing, Bath Road, Chippenham, Wilts; *Stamps and Ships* by James C. Watson, published by Faber & Faber, London, 1962. *Mail Ships of the Channel Islands* by Richard Mayne, published by Picton Publishing as previous; *Ships and Stamps, a Guide*, published by the National Postal Museum, London.

SPACE
Space Catalogue by Bernard Lollini, published by Harris Publications Ltd, London; *Stamps Tell the Story of Space Travel* by Kelen Emery, published by Nelson, Nashville, USA, 1972; *The Astrophile*, published by the Space Unit of the ATA (see Item 3 for particulars). *Study of Suspect Space Covers* by Dr Ramkissoon and Lester E. Winnick, published by the Space Unit of the ATA.

SPORTS
Encylopedia of Sports Stamps by Robert Bateman, published by Stanley Paul Ltd, London, 1969; *Sports Stamps* by Carlo Enhagen, published by Stanley Paul Ltd, London, 1961; *Ball Games on Stamps* by Juegos de Pelota and Los Selos, published in Montevideo, 1968; *Timbres et Sports Catalogue*, published by Guy Depolier, Paris, 1949; *Cycling and Postage Stamps* by A. E. Gould, published by Capen, Ipswich.

STAMPS
Stamps in Schools by the Postal Publicity Branch, Post Office, London; 'Stamps on Stamps', published by the Crown Agents in the *Thematic Guide*, 1952–64.

UNITED NATIONS
UN & Related World Wide Stamps, checklist, Study 4 by the United Nations Study Group, *Borek Stamp Catalogue UN*, published by Richard Borek, Federal Republic of Germany, 1978; *Postal Issues of the UN 1951–72*, published by the UN

Postal Administration, UN, New York; *UN: Twelve Philatelic Years 1945–57*, with supplements to 1967 by Marian Carne Zinsmeister, published by Van Dahl Publications Inc., Oregon, USA.

UNIVERSAL POSTAL UNION
The 37th Aniversary Issues by Marian Carne Zinsmeister, published by the Society of Philatelic Americans, Illinois, USA.

WAR
Allied Postage Stamps of War 1914–25, published by David Field, London, 1932; *Postage Stamps of War* by Douglas B. Armstrong, published by Stamp Collecting, London.

ZOOLOGY
Zoology on Postage Stamps by R. Dennis Way and O. D. Standen, published by Harvey & Blythe, London, 1951.

General books on stamp collecting
Collecting Stamps by Eric Smith, published by Batsford, London, 1966; *How to Arrange and Write up a Stamp Collection* by Stanley Phillips & C. P. Rang, published by Stanley Gibbons, London, 1966; *The Standard Guide to Stamp Collecting* by Scott Coins & Stamp Co., New York, 1938.

General and Specialist Societies

General

The British Philatelic Federation and the National Philatelic Society, 1 Whitehall Place, London, SW1A 2HE; The American Philatelic Society, PO Box 800, State College, Pennsylvania 16801, USA; Inter-American Philatelic Federation, Commissioner for Thematics, Mrs Barbara Williams de Violini, PO Box 5025, Oxnard, California 93031, USA.

Of special note for all thematic collectors is the American Topical Association, 3306 North 50th Street, Milwaukee, Wisconsin 53216, USA. This organisation is international with 10,000 members in 90 different countries. It publishes a 100 page bi-monthly illustrated journal *Topical Time*, a nearly 200 page membership directory, has a 687 member information board to answer queries on 353 topics free of charge. It has a free translation service for 27 languages. Dues are nominal. At the current date it has 41 specialised study units, each of which is open to anyone interested in the subject of each unit. Initial information about each unit and which is listed in the *Directory of ATA Study Units* can be obtained from Donald W. Smith, 1633 Florida Avenue, Johnstown, Pennsylvania 15402, USA.

Specialist

The Alba Stamp Group (Scotland); The Fine Arts Philatelist, Jewell Sonderegger, PO Box 1606, Midland, Michigan 48640, USA; The Guild of St Gabriel (Religion) Great Britain and Ireland, Miss M. Mansfield, 47 Grosvenor Road, Wallington, Surrey SM6 0EN, England; The Philatelic Music Circle (Music), Mrs Gwyneth Williams, 3 Lydstep House, Bishops Close, Whitchurch, Cardiff CF4 1PE, Wales; The Methodist

Philatelic Society (Methodism), L. Hebditch, 27 Kingsmead Close, Arle, Cheltenham GL51 0AW, England; Pertohil (Petroleum), 2808 Bayley Street, Bakersfield, California 93305, USA; Collectors of Religion on Stamps (COROS), Mrs Viola Esau, 600 West Orange Grove G184, Tucson, Arizona 65704, USA.

Index